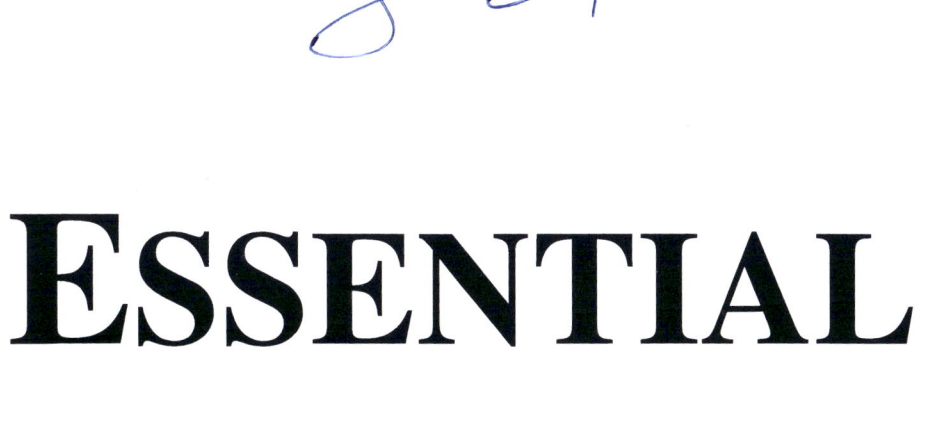

ESSENTIAL GOLF

Everything you need to know
And how to learn it!

By John Dunigan

Golf Better Productions
Hockessin, DE

ESSENTIAL GOLF

ESSENTIAL GOLF. First printing. Copyright © 1998 by John Dunigan. Printed and bound in the United States of America. All rights reserved. No part of this book may be reproduced in any form or by any electronic or mechanical means including information storage and retrieval systems without permission in writing from the publisher, except by a reviewer, who may quote brief passages in a review. Published by **Golf Better Productions** PO Box 1557 Hockessin, DE 19707.

ISBN 0-9669375-0-3

Library of Congress Catalog Card Number: 98-96930

Acknowledgments

To my golf students. Because of you, this book is possible. You have taught me far more than I can say. In fact, I'm not really sure who the teacher is.

I wish to thank Dick Dubroff of FINAL FOCUS in Wilmington, DE for his superb work on the cover photos and full swing sequence digital photos.

Special thanks goes to Davis Sezna from Hartefeld National Golf Course in Avondale, PA for allowing us full range of his wonderful golf course, where we took our photos. Hartefeld National is an outstanding golf course of inspiring beauty. It is as delightful to look at as it is to play.

I'd like to thank Randy Rhomberg and *Cleveland Golf* for making terrific golf clubs. If you're in the market for new weapons, give them a look.

My teaching has been significantly influenced by so many people that it's difficult to list them all. I feel compelled to mention these people because I am forever in debt to them. It would be misleading, not to mention dishonest, for me to lead you to believe that I had no help in learning what I know.

Mike Bender, who is one of the most knowledgeable people in the world on the golf swing, helped me considerably with my own swing. Chuck Hogan has been a major influence on the way I teach golf. His work with the LPGA Urban Youth Golf Program has opened my mind and forced me to constantly evaluate what I teach and how I teach it. I've watched Craig Shankland give more golf clinics than I can count. He's wonderful to watch at work. Dave Pelz's study of the short game has probably influenced every golfer in the world, whether they know it or not. Lynn Marriot, whom I've also met through the LPGA Program, is another brilliant teacher I have learned from. Anything you can get your hands on by Joseph Chilton Pearce will change your life. The willingness of these people to share what they know with us is impressive and all too rare in this competitive world. I'd like to thank these folks for making golf a better game and for making the world a better place.

I'd like to thank all my friends for their support and aid with editing and digital photography. To Joe Schulte, Samantha Keith, Billy Dickinson, Christy Sculley, Bill Tansey, Kelley Tindall, Amanda Bernard, Carolyn Chamberlain, Abbie McCammon, Karla Kirkbride, Roger London and Andrew VonDeak: Thank you for your time, energy, and immense help, I could not have done it without you.

Last but certainly not least, many thanks go to Mike and Don Brewer and Shonda and Curt Schilling of the Schilling Golf Center in Kennett Square, PA for giving me a great facility at which to teach golf.

DEDICATION

This book is dedicated to Grace Dunigan, my Mom. She's quite a lady. Thanks for putting up with me all those years when I thought I knew all the answers.

TO CONTACT THE AUTHOR

E-mail at essentialgolf@erols.com or write John Dunigan at Golf Better Productions PO Box 1557 Hockessin, DE 19707. Your comments, good or bad, are welcomed and appreciated.

PREFACE

WHY YOU NEED THIS BOOK

If you want to learn or improve your golf, you must not only know *what* to do, more importantly, you need to know *how to learn* what to do so that you avoid or change the bad habits that make golf more difficult than it really is.

If you are a new golfer, don't even think of starting out without some guidance. On your own, this game may take you forever to learn, but it doesn't have to happen like that.

If you have been golfing for some time, you might be pretty frustrated with golf. LISTEN. The average golf score has not improved in twenty years, largely because golf has been taught improperly, and learned even worse. This book will clear up some of the misinformation which has made golf such a mystery to the average golfer. Well, there is no magic involved. There are no secrets. The application of some basic principles is what the game is about. Unfortunately, those basic principles are often misunderstood and misinterpreted. This book makes sense out of the nonsense.

Golf is not really all that difficult, but it is a bit of a struggle to learn all that there is to know. However, the guided struggle is far better than the blind struggle. This book is your guide to good golf.

My plan is to give you a complete understanding of golf, so that you can become your own coach. I wrote this book precisely because I think you can play this game well *if* you learn it correctly. I am going to teach you exactly what you need to know, and I'm going to tell you exactly how to learn it. All you have to do is follow instructions.

This book is written mainly for the beginning to advanced intermediate golfer in search of a better way to learn, practice, and play the game. If you are frustrated, you will find what you need to make golf fun again. You will find the instruction simple, clear and very effective, but don't kid yourself. You will have to apply yourself to learn it.

I am very excited about this book because I know it will make golf easier for you. You'll quickly improve and enjoy the process. This book will help you immensely, and *that's* why you need it!

Fore! Word

How to use this book

This book is designed as your guide, so keep your guide with you when you practice golf. I have written for the right handed golfer, so if you are left handed, reverse the rights and lefts throughout. First of all, study the pictures and try to absorb them into your mind. Close your eyes after studying them for a while. Can you see the pictures in your mind's eye? All learning occurs through a model, so you need to get clear pictures in your head to serve as your model before you attempt to learn the movements. If you are not clear in your mind, your mind certainly can't tell your body what to do.

Once you have a crystal clear picture in your head, then pick up the club. Begin very slowly and *without a ball*, try to match the pictures. Smooth out the motion until you can flow through the backswing and forward swing without a hitch. Begin to feel how the motion is designed to send your energy, through the club head, toward the target. Relate the swing to the target. Think "this is what it feels like to swing to the target." Put a ball down and make the same swing toward the target, and just let the ball get in the way. Make no effort to hit the ball. Simply make your swing until you find the ball with it. Watch out for trying to hit the ball. You can ruin your swing real fast. I suggest that you go very slowly when you first put a ball down and concentrate totally on making the correct swing. If you hit the ball, that's fine. If you don't, that's fine too. Don't worry about contact, it'll come with experience.

You have to know your swing in your mind first, and then teach it to your body. I guarantee that you will be able to teach yourself better if you go slowly. As your hands learn where to go, you will become increasingly comfortable with, and proficient at, the motion. As you have to work less to make the right motion, you will naturally increase your speed. Don't rush the speed. You'll learn bad habits and then you'll have to come see me, and that's a lot more expensive than this book.

When your mechanics are set (which you can do at home), go to the range or putting green, book in hand, and start on the drills. Begin the process of educating your hands, and then go Play Golf. Get feedback from the golf course on where you need improvement, and consult the book for how to proceed. It's all here. Go to it.

Contents

Preface
Fore! Word
Introduction 1
   Some Common Misconceptions About Golf 4
   How to Improve Your Golf 6
   Right Practice 7
   Before You Swing 9
   Important Terms 12

1 Putting 17
   The Putting Hold 18
   Putting Setup 19
   The Iron Triangle 20
   The Iron Triangle Putt 21
   The Push 22
   The Putting Track 23
   The Pre-Shot Routine, Part 1 26
   The One Footer 28
   Aiming Exercise 29
   Reading Greens 30
   Three Ball 32
   Twelve Ball 33
   Around the World 34
   North, South, East, and West 35
   The Twenty Footer 36

2 Chipping 39
   The Full Swing Hold 40
   Chipping Setup 44
   The Iron Triangle Chip 46
   The Long Club 47
   Downward Contact 48
   Pick a Spot 49
   Up and Down 50

3 PITCHING 53
- Address Position 54
- The Push 58
- The Half and Half Swing 60
- Full Swing Address and Pitching Address 62
- The Three Quarter Backswing 64
- The Three Quarter and Half Swing 66
- Keys to the Three Quarter and Half Swing 68
- Make Your Practice Count 69

4 THE FULL SWING 73
- The Importance of a Model 74
- 7 Steps to Good Golf 75
- The Turn 76
- The Level Turn 78
- Address Position Turn Drill 80
- The Belly Button Drill 81
- The Full Backswing 82
- At the Top 84
- The Forward Swing 85
- Forward Swing Keys 86
- How to Practice Your Forward Swing 88
- Mastering the Forward Swing 89
- The Release 90
- The Full and Half Swing 92
- The Finish 94
- Late Speed 96
- Full Swing Sequences 98
- The Four Keys to the Essential Golf Swing 106
- The Swing Plane 110
- Watch Out for These Mistakes 114

5 FULL SWING DRILLS 117
- The Level Swing 118
- The Foot High Swing 120
- The Swinging Start 122
- Feet Together 123
- Right Foot Out 124

Left Foot Out 125
Right Hand Only 126

6 PRACTICING GOLF 127
What Are All These Clubs for, Anyway? 128
Approaching the Ball and the Waggle 130
Ball Position 131
Posture 132
Contact.. 133
The Right Clubs for You 134
Ball Flight Control 135
Ball Flight Laws Quiz 137
Educated Hands 139
How to Practice Golf.. 140
Pre-Shot Routine, Part 2 142
Recommended Practice Routine 143
Tempo 146

7 DIFFERENT LIES 147
Downhill 148
Uphill 149
Sidehill, Above Your Feet 150
Sidehill, Below Your Feet 150
Rough 151
Tight Lies 152
In a Divot 152
Sand Play 153
The Slider 154
The Rake Line 155
Where to Enter The Sand...................................... 156
The Explosion 157
Fairway Bunkers 158

8 PLAYING GOLF 159
Etiquette 160
Golf: The Mind Game 165

9 TROUBLESHOOTING 173

INTRODUCTION

Congratulations, you have just purchased the only golf instruction book you will ever need. Many golfers will lead you to believe that golf is unbearably difficult and frustrating. Well, it's not *easy*, but if you use the information contained in these pages, you will understand the mechanics of the full swing, the short game, specialty shots, and the mental game, *and* you will learn a method of practicing that will make golf much easier for you and help you shoot lower scores almost immediately.

I wrote this book because I am dismayed that golfers, after having taken lessons from other teachers, spent thousands of dollars on golf schools, and read all kinds of golf books, still do not understand how golf works. I want to change that. I don't blame the students. The teacher is almost always to blame when a student doesn't "get it." Think about this: 80% of all golfers slice the ball. I believe that the reason for that is that they are doing just what they have been taught. It is true that golfers make the game more difficult by practicing in a way that almost ensures that they don't improve, but they just need to understand how important it is to practice correctly. This book will solve both problems.

I am frustrated by golf instruction which has gotten far too complex and difficult for the average player to even understand, let alone master. Sometimes, what is appropriate for the touring pro is simply much too difficult for the average person to learn. When is the last time you hit five or six hundred balls a day for a few *years*? I intend to make golf much simpler for you.

Additionally, I have had it up to here with the golf equipment industry's empty promises about how this ball or that set of irons or this $500 driver is going to change your game forever. Do you really think you can buy a game? You'd be far better off if you'd sink your money into a video camera, so that you can use this book and teach yourself golf the right way. Then you won't need new clubs 'till the old ones wear out.

LISTEN. Golf is not as difficult as you think. Playing the game for a living is difficult. I've tried that, and let me tell you it's *tough*. But playing respectably and continually improving your game is pretty easy, if you have the patience to learn correctly. Playing good golf is *much* easier if you have the following:

- Clear pictures in your mind that will serve as models for the short game and the full swing mechanics you will need to play golf.

- A method of practicing that ensures you become the model.

- An understanding of what makes a ball fly the way it does.
- A complete learning program which covers all aspects of the game, both mental and physical, so that you learn not only the mechanics of golf, but also how to score.

Essential Golf gives you all of the above.

Although you will find a revolutionary approach to the full swing in this book, I want to make it clear that the full swing is only a small part of golf. Golf is about getting the ball in the hole in the least number of strokes possible, therefore, *Essential Golf* also includes what you *must* know about putting, chipping, pitching and sand play. You will be able to build a complete game with this book as your guide.

Part of the problem with golf is that you don't know *what* to learn in the first place. There is so much instructional material out there it's scary, and the content of the material varies wildly in an often contradictory way which leads to total confusion for people trying to learn golf. All learning occurs through a model. You could not write the letter "A" without a model of an "A" in your mind. You *need* a model. If you are like most golfers, you have several opposing ideas (models) about the golf swing. Rather than becoming a student of the game, with more technical knowledge than ability to use it, you need to stick to one model until you learn it, and ignore all others. By embracing a model and working toward it, you rid yourself of the paralyzing indecision most golfers face on every shot: "Which swing should I use this time?" It will help to know that the full swing model in this book is as close to the perfect swing as you can get.

The second part of your problem is that you must practice correctly so that you learn the correct mechanics. Most golfers, and I don't mean just the bad ones, do not know how to practice well. Far too many golfers approach golf the wrong way right from the start. You probably did the same thing I did: went to the range and smashed balls around until you ran out of balls or quit from frustration. The problem is that darned ball. If you put the ball in the way too soon, you'll try to hit it. Yes, I meant to say that. Rather than make a swing designed to send the ball to a target, you'll make a swing designed to hit the ball. These two swings are very different. The swing designed to hit the ball doesn't go toward the target. Want the ball to go to the target? Well a good place to start is to swing toward the target!

So many golfers rely only on their sense of feel to tell them that their mechanics are correct. If it feels good, it must be good, right? Wrong. Way wrong! The mechanics must precede the feel. Most often, it's not even close, and that's dangerous. You must get the mechanics correct first, and then learn how those mechanics feel or you'll most certainly learn incorrectly. Mechanics first, feel later. Please don't forget that!

Most people also make the vital mistake of working on one thing and then evaluating something entirely different. You may have done the same. There you are on the range, working on your swing, but instead of evaluating your swing itself, you intently watch the ball fly in order to determine whether you made the right swing. The truth is, you may *think* that you are making the right move, but unless you have some kind of feedback (video is the best), you really don't have any idea what you are actually doing.

The last part of your problem may be that you have not committed yourself to learning the game. Golf is not like tennis. In tennis, you can jump on the court and within a short amount of time, get the ball going back and forth well enough to have a blast. Not so in golf. You are going to have to pay some dues first. The good news is that if you learn correctly the first time, you can seriously shorten the dues paying period. But you are definitely not going to escape it altogether.

This book is designed to be a complete guide to learning golf. Everything that you will find in these pages is essential. No band-aids or quick fixes or unnecessary complications, just the fundamentals. That's where the name comes from. Further, I don't just tell you to do something, I teach you *how* to learn it. Although I may contradict some old, standard methods of teaching, you will find that what I teach you makes perfect common sense, and that *you can do it*. You will get a model for every part of the game; drills to help you habituate good mechanics; and you will learn how to bring your new skills to the golf course. In other words, you will get a complete learning package. This book is all you need.

Ask yourself these questions: Are you getting better? Are you happy with your progress? Do you understand golf? Do you know what you are supposed to look like? Do you know what makes the ball do what it does? Do you get the most out of your practice time? Chances are that if you picked up this book, you need some help. Help is here.

I don't think there is another book out there that is as complete or as thorough in its instruction. I sincerely believe that this book will be of great value to you.

Happy Learning,

John Dunigan

Some Common Misconceptions About Golf

Misconception #1

You can learn golf or make changes swinging the club at full speed.

Feel is not real. At full speed, you may *feel* that you are making a new move, but the *reality* is that you will do the same old move unless you slow down. Full speed happens too fast for conscious control, so whatever habits you have will show up when you go full speed. I see this all the time. Even my own students will sometimes practice only at full speed between lessons and not improve as much as they could have. The inevitable result is that the next lesson is the same as the last one.

I constantly implore my students to slow down so that the club does not move faster than their brain. Your mind must be fully aware of what's moving when and where the club is throughout the motion. I have my students say out loud the keys to their swing *as they go through them* to create and increase their conscious awareness of their swing.

The speed at which my students learn when they do go slowly continually amazes me. This approach should be taken for all stroke mechanics in this book.

Misconception #2

Body turn, whether hips or shoulders, starts the forward swing.

Earlier, I mentioned that 80% of the golfers in the world slice the ball. The reason can be directly traced to the erroneous instruction that body turn should start the forward swing. In the full swing chapter of this book, you will find a section on the swing plane that will show you very clearly that if you do start the forward swing with your body, your hands will follow your body and move away from, rather than toward the plane. The result is that your club will not swing toward the target as you move through impact. Instead, it will move left of the target unless you manage to correct yourself in mid-swing. Unfortunately, this move is still widely taught. Good luck to you if you decide to do it.

Misconception #3

Power comes from your legs, hips or body.

Believe it or not, the number one power accumulator in the golf swing is your right arm, for right handed golfers. With a small computer that measured club head speed, I hit five iron shots with my normal effort swing. My club head speed was consistently around 90 m.p.h.. Then I hit the same club but with only my right hand on the club. My club head speed was consistently around 73 m.p.h.. *With one hand!* That means that *eighty- one percent* of my club head speed comes from my right arm/hand. As an example, I hit my seven iron 160 yards with my normal swing. With my right hand only, I hit it about 130 yards. Interesting, huh? By the way, I'm not very strong at all. A one hundred pound bench press is about all I can handle.

Misconception #4

Weight shift adds distance to your golf shots.

I did a little study on my friend's golf computer in Daytona Beach, FL. I wanted to find out the relationship between weight shift and club head speed, so I spent three hours on this computer that tracked weight shift, club head speed, club path and club face angle. Club head speed is the most important determinant of distance. I hit drivers, varying the amount of weight shift from just about zero, up to seventy percent on the backswing, to seventy percent on the forward swing (at impact that is, not at the finish). What I found was that the difference in club head speed between zero weight shift and seventy percent weight shift was approximately *one mile per hour*. One mile per hour is worth only about 2.33 yards, which I find to be insignificant. The real news is that the more I shifted my weight, the farther off line my club path and face angle were, creating amazingly less control, with very little additional distance. That's not a wise trade-off.

Misconception #5

Keep your head still.

This is a dangerous misconception because if you attempt to keep your head perfectly still, you will not be able to make a proper backswing turn, which will set you up for failure right from the start of your swing. Allow your head to turn a little to the right and move as much as two inches to the right as you make your backswing. The important thing is to make sure that you don't straighten up your spine angle as you swing, not that you keep your head still.

Misconception #6

I picked my head up.

I can't tell you how many times I have heard golfers say exactly this after missing a shot completely, or rolling a shot along the ground. Picking your head up is almost never the problem here. The way to miss or roll a shot is to stand up as you make the backswing, or bend your arms as you swing the club through impact.

Misconception #7

Keep your hands passive, and let your body control the club.

The club is not stuck to your belly button, it's stuck in your hands. Need I say more?

How to Improve Your Golf

Improving your golf game is all in your head. Saying you want to improve (or learn for the first time) is the easy part. The hard part is backing up your words with commitment. You must realize that, in the beginning, you will have to grind through the initiation period that all of us have had to go through. You don't just start out good at this game. You have to earn it. There are no natural golfers, the good ones just look natural because they have stuck with it through the inevitable ups and downs that make this game such a challenge. Realize now that no one has ever mastered the game. The best players in the world have all had times when they felt they could do no wrong and times then they felt the opposite. The key is to hang in there when you seem to take steps backward, because you are not far from leaping forward. Anyone can play this game. You don't need fantastic natural talent. More than anything, you need persistence. And some good instruction.

You have to discipline yourself to practice correctly. What is good practice? Good practice entails knowing *what* to practice, *why* to practice it and *how* to practice it. You must concentrate on exactly what you are working on, whether it is your swing mechanics or your ball flight, and then evaluate only what you are working on. Finally, you must be able to apply your knowledge on the golf course, in all types of situations, and under all sorts of conditions. Learn to Play Golf. That's the whole point of this book.

Get fascinated by the process of golfing and what makes a ball do what it does. It's not that difficult. You can do it. You just have to learn and put to use, a few fundamental motions, and you are on your way. Go slowly. Get the mechanics down first. Then add the ball. I can't say that enough.

This is going to take some time. There is just *so much* to learn. The fundamentals are actually easy, but the variety of shots you need to play the game requires quite a lot of learning before you can "just do it." That's OK. Just take your time. Realize that you are headed in the right direction, and you'll be fine. This book is your guide.

RIGHT PRACTICE

We all want to be better immediately, but that's not possible. What is possible is that if you practice correctly and do your homework, you can quickly own a swing to be proud of and be well on your way to hitting controlled, powerful shots. However, that's not all there is to golf, you must have a good short game. If you work on your short game as shown in this book, you will continually improve your ability to get the ball in the hole. Of course, as with anything, how fast you improve depends upon the quality and frequency of your practice. Here are a few Rules of Right Practice which you would do well to follow.

RULE #1 BE NICE TO YOURSELF.

I'm serious. Be your own best friend. Talk to yourself in a nurturing, helpful, positive way. Have you ever called yourself stupid for hitting a bad shot? Don't. Maintain your self esteem and your sense of humor. It *is* just a game isn't it?

RULE #2 IF YOU WANT TO IMPROVE YOUR SWING, SLOW DOWN AND FORGET ABOUT CONTACT.

Again, I am serious. If you want to improve your swing, concentrate on your swing, not contact. If you attempt to focus on both swing and contact at the same time, you will get neither, and that's no fun. Practice your swing and make sure it is correct. You will have to slow way down to make a good swing, and that's OK. Your brain will learn whatever you teach it, whether you go fast or slow. So if you want to learn the correct swing, practice slowly and perfectly, and gradually add speed later. Contact is easy. When your swing is ready, contact will be a matter of simple adjustment. If the swing is not there first, contact could be a real problem.

RULE #3 REMOVE THE WORD "BAD" FROM YOUR VOCABULARY.

Once you are ready to start hitting balls, watch your shots closely until the ball stops rolling. Become very interested in where the ball goes, but do not judge undesirable results as bad. There is no failure, only feedback. You swing, the ball goes somewhere, you say "Hmm, interesting," and you try again. For instance, if you make a swing and determine that you made a club path error, instantly forget the shot, and take a couple of practice swings with the perfect club path to remind yourself of what you wanted to do. Immediately replace an errant swing with the right swing and tell yourself "That's the swing!"

You need to enjoy your good shots. Get psyched about them. That which you give more attention to becomes more strongly imprinted in your mind, so store only the results you want to repeat. Now I don't mean you have to celebrate with champagne every time you hit a good shot, but most certainly you should give yourself a big smile and congratulate yourself. Don't just assume that you *should* hit 'em that way.

RULE #4 TRY AND TRY AGAIN.

Once you learn to swing well, you have to "trial and error it" until you are able to make good contact, swing the club in the right direction or putt or chip the ball the right distance. It's easy. Adjust. Do not make the same mistake over and over again. You won't have fun, and you won't learn as fast.

RULE #5 HAVE FUN!

Golf is a game, and games are for fun. Right? So have fun. Have fun learning and experimenting with all the facets of the game. Have fun making mistakes. Mistakes are good because they point out weaknesses in your game which, when improved, will make you a better golfer. Walk whenever you can and have fun getting exercise among the beautiful scenery.

RULE #6 USE A MIRROR.

When you are working on your full swing, you will *need* to practice in front of a mirror and without a ball. You must have a feedback mechanism so you can be certain that you are practicing correctly. Do not trust your feel, your feel is just not accurate. If you have a video camera, that works great. You will learn your swing in a matter of weeks if you spend at least fifteen minutes per day practicing in front of a mirror. Don't practice making mistakes, USE A MIRROR!

RULE #7 BE NICE TO YOURSELF!

See Rule #1. I mean it.

BEFORE YOU SWING

First you'll need a club. For now, a putter and a sand wedge or pitching wedge will do, but in a short while, you will need clubs that fit you well. Here's a *general* guideline: Men taller than six feet-one, may need longer than standard, men's clubs. Women with good hand and arm strength who are five feet-eight, or taller, probably should use men's standard length clubs. Women under five feet-seven may need ladies length clubs. Women around five feet and under may need petite clubs. It is important to have shafts which fit your size and swing. You will find it easier to hit good shots. Please have a knowledgeable club fitter set you up with the right shaft length and flex, the correct grip size, and the proper lie angle. You'll be happy you did.

Juniors should have either ladies clubs (for taller youngsters), or their own junior clubs. Junior clubs have lighter shafts and club heads than adult clubs which have been cut down, making them easier to swing. Use a junior set if possible. Your children will have more success hitting the ball, and success makes golf more fun. Actually, that goes for golfers of all ages, doesn't it?

ON GOLF CLUBS:
Nowadays, it is almost impossible to buy a new set of "bad" irons. The golf industry has reached a state where iron head technology is about as good as it can get. You can buy an excellent set of irons for about $200 which will be almost, if not just, as good as a $700 or $800 set. The key is getting clubs that fit *you*.

Driver technology is still improving, but I do not see how club manufacturers are going to improve much at all on the titanium drivers that are available now. I do believe that the titanium drivers are the best drivers ever offered (note that the best players in the world overwhelmingly use titanium). The benefit is not raw distance, however. What you get with titanium is a bigger "effective hitting surface," not a bigger "sweetspot." Basically, the real difference between today's drivers and the old ones is that your mis-hits will go straighter, and therefore they will *play* as if you hit them longer. Shots hit on the sweetspot do not go any farther with the new stuff. But of course, golf is a game of minimizing the severity of your missed shots, and your misses will be better with the new drivers.

To make things a little more confusing, I prefer smaller headed, not-necessarily-titanium, fairway woods because they are easier to hit from the rough and other imperfect lies. Bigger heads are a little less manageable in difficult lies, but they're great when the ball's on a tee.

The Graphite Question:

Do you need graphite shafts? You will be hard pressed to find steel shafted drivers and fairway woods these days, but I'm not sure why. For some reason, the golf industry wants you to believe that graphite plays better, but I'm not convinced. The reason is torque. Torque refers to the club shaft's resistance to twisting. The greater a shaft's torque, the more it twists. The club head is attached to the shaft, and so when the shaft twists, the club head will turn in the same direction, and that can't be good.

So what am I torquing about? (sorry, I couldn't resist). If you swing the club slowly, the lightness of graphite shafts may help you get a little more club head speed, but if you swing the club quickly, perhaps at club head speeds of eighty m.p.h. or more with a five iron, the same graphite shaft will twist (at the most critical moment in the golf swing; impact) significantly more than a steel shaft, sending the ball farther off line than it should have gone. Steel shafts are also easier to match than graphite, so steel shafted irons will perform more consistently through the set than graphite shafted irons. For these reasons, I feel very confident telling you that steel shafts play better than graphite, at least in the irons. The only positive statements I can make for graphite is that it is lighter and perhaps a little easier to swing. It does damp vibration more than steel, making it more suitable for players who either lack swing speed, or have elbow or other arm problems which could be exacerbated by shock and vibration at impact. As far as woods go, however, since you will find it very difficult to find steel shafted woods, you will have to search for woods that come with low torque shafts. Additionally, it may not be as difficult to find reasonably similar wood shafts because you'll probably have only a Driver, 3 Wood and 5 Wood in your bag, as opposed to nine or ten irons. If you want a really good graphite shaft, you're going to have to pay for it. They start at about $100, just for the shaft.

Buying Clubs:

LISTEN. If you are just starting out in golf, it makes very little sense to go out and spend $800 on a set of irons and then spend another $300 or so *each* for woods. In the first place, you are going to give whatever clubs you buy quite a beating in your first year of golf, and in the second place, you almost certainly could not tell the difference between a $200 set of irons and an $800 set anyway. My point is: save your money (for now) and get stainless steel irons with steel shafts and, after you go through this book, get the clubs fit to you. Proper fitting may include having the club heads bent into the correct "lie" for your swing, (don't worry about bending the clubs, it's very common). You will want to have your swing mechanics owned before you get your clubs fit to you. Otherwise, you may have to have them altered again.

You do not have to buy a titanium driver right away. Remember, you are going to have to learn to make good contact through trial and error. It makes more sense to trial and error it with less expensive clubs. After you get your swing ironed out and make good contact regularly, then you may want to upgrade to titanium. You don't want to pay $350 for one club and then ruin it, do you? If money is not important, you can ignore the above.

Beware the "used car type" Sales Person

I'd like to think that all salespeople are honest, but... You have to watch out for promises about the magic a new set of clubs will work for you. You already know what I think about shafts, but don't forget what I said about club heads: Whatever you get these days is going to be very similar to every other set out there. Once you get clubs that fit you, they will *all* perform very much alike.

Now don't go thinking that some club is going to transform your game. That's just not true. You can't buy a golf game. All you can do is buy the best equipment you can afford, and make sure it fits you. Swinging the thing is up to you.

I remember an unsatisfied customer who demanded his money back because his new wedge hit the ball fat and thin, as if the club had a mind of its own. I could only laugh.

One last thing. If you are going to buy a "starter set," which is probably a good idea, please make sure that the club heads are stainless steel. I have seen many alloy club heads break because they were just plain cheap. If the word "stainless" is not printed on the club heads of a low price set, ask if they are stainless, and be wary if they are not.

You can also assemble a starter set of your own. Good clubs to have are a Sand wedge, 9 Iron, 7 Iron, 5 Iron, 3 Wood, and Putter.

Important Terms

Before we move on to the good stuff, there are some terms with which you should be familiar, so that we speak the same language. Everything is explained for a right-handed player. Just reverse the rights and lefts if you are left-handed. These are not in alphabetical order, they're more in golf order.

These are terms you need to know now, to help you learn. They will be used throughout the book.

Target line. A straight line drawn between the ball and the target.

Square. Aiming at the target (as in square club face) or parallel to the target line (as in square stance).

Club face angle. The direction in which a perpendicular line from the center of your club face would point at impact. Can be either **square** (line points to the target), **open** (line points to the right), or **closed** (line points to the left).

Club path. The direction in which you swing the club through impact. Can be either **inside-out**, or **outside-in** for the full swing.

Inside-out. The club head traveling in an arc from the left of the target line, out to the right as it approaches the ball. Stand behind the ball and imagine the target line (the line running from the ball to the target). To the left of the target line is inside. To the right is outside. **Inside-out** is how you are designed to swing and how the golf club is designed to be swung.

Outside-in. The club traveling from the right of the target line, across and to the left of it through impact. Known as a **pull**, this is the path which results in the dreaded slice.

CLUB PATH AND CLUB FACE ANGLE ARE THE TWO MAJOR FACTORS THAT INFLUENCE THE FLIGHT OF THE BALL.

Stance line. A straight line drawn across the tips of toes. Can be either **square** (parallel to the target line), **open** (to the right of the target line), or **closed** (to the left of the target line).

Shoulder line. The line across the front of your shoulders.

Address position. How you stand over the ball. Includes your posture, alignment, and ball position.

Ball position. Where the ball is in your stance, relative to your feet.

Alignment. You are aligned to the target when your stance line, shoulders, hips, and forearms are all parallel to the target line.

Club and ball terms.

Club head. The whole thing at the end of the long skinny tube called a **shaft**.

Club face. The relatively flat, "front" of the thing at the end of the shaft, that's designed to hit the ball.

Hosel. The part of the club head where the shaft is inserted.

Heel. The end of the club head nearest to the hosel.

Toe. The other end.

Iron. The sharp edged metal headed clubs in a set.

Wedge. The most lofted irons in a set. Designed for hitting short shots that stop quickly. There are four types of wedges. In order of most lofted: Lob, Sand, Gap, and Pitching. You only need a sand wedge or pitching wedge for now. The pitching wedge used to be used for pitching, hence the name. Since then, the sand wedge has come along to take the pitching wedge's job, so the pitching wedge is more like a #10 iron, rather than a club used to hit pitch shots.

Wood. Seldom made of wood anymore. These are big headed clubs made for hitting your longest shots.

Driver. The longest of the woods. Use it to tee off on long holes.

Fairway wood. There are several, from a #3 to a #15. You'll probably find a set that comes with a driver, #3 wood and #5 wood. The #3 wood works great as a driver. A fairway wood with a number higher than #5 is considered a **utility wood**.

Pull. A ball that starts left of the target.

Push. A ball that starts right of the target.

Slice. A ball that makes a big curve to the right.

Fade. A small slice.

Hook. A ball that makes a big curve to the left.

Draw. A small hook.

Pull-hook. A ball that starts left and hooks.

Pull-slice. A ball that starts left and slices.

Push-hook. A ball that starts right of the target and hooks.

Push-slice. A ball that starts right of the target and slices.

Thin shot, aka skinny. Hitting just a little too high on the ball, making it fly lower than normal. Thin shots can turn out very well. That's called "thin to win," although your hands may sting a little.

Fat shot, aka chunky. Hitting the big ball (Earth) before you hit the ball. When you hit behind the ball, you have hit a **fat** shot. Also referred to as "heavy."

Topped shot, aka worm burner. Hitting the top of the ball, causing it to roll along the ground.

Shank. Hitting the ball with the hosel instead of the club face. The ball goes dead right. The only response is to say "Shank you very much."

The rest of these terms will clue you in as far as golf course talk goes.

Tee, aka peg. A little wooden stick that looks like a nail, on which you place your ball before hitting **a tee shot** (first shot on a hole) from the **tee box**. Put your ball on the tee first, before trying to push the tee into the ground.

Tee box. Usually defined by different colored markers between which you should tee your ball. Depending on how long you want the course to play, you can choose to play from any set of tees. The red tees are usually most forward (shortest). The whites are usually in the middle. And the blues are back farthest from the hole.

Par. The score an *expert* player would be expected to make on a hole. Not yet being an expert, you may want to make up your own definition of par, and evaluate your game by that. There are par 3's, par 4's, and par 5's, and you could be par for the course, or so many over or under par.

Bogey. One more than par.

Birdie. One less than par.

Eagle. Two less than par.

Range. The driving range. Better said, the practice field. Where you learn the **mechanics** of the golf swing and ball flight control to prepare to play golf. Prepare is a better word than practice.

Golf course. Where you play/learn **golf**. Definitely **not** where you learn or practice mechanics.

Practice green. Where you experiment to find out how you best get the ball into the hole. Ask someone in the pro shop if you are allowed to chip before you do.

Putting green. Where you do your best to get the ball into the hole. Please be careful when walking on this most hallowed of golfing ground.

Fringe, aka apron. A (twelve to twenty-four inch wide) strip of approximately 3/4 inch grass that surrounds the putting green. It separates the green from the rough and the fairway.

Fairway. The short grass between the tee box and the green. Try to hit it.

Rough. The high grass surrounding the fairway and the green.

Divot. The piece of ground dug up (sometimes) when you hit the ball. Please replace it so that it can grow back.

Ball mark. The indentation in the putting green made when the ball hits it. Fix it by using a tool made for the purpose, or by using a tee to pull the ground back into place. Tap the mark with the sole of your putter to smooth it out.

Green in regulation. The expert golfer is expected to be on the green of a par 3 in one shot, two shots for a par 4, and three shots for a par 5.

Bunker, aka trap. A hollowed out area of ground usually filled with sand, but sometimes just rough. Sand bunkers are more common than grass.

Hazard. Water and sand. Specific rules apply as to proper procedure. Please consult a rules book. Red or yellow stakes define water hazards.

Out of bounds, aka OB. Off the golf course. Defined by white stakes. Don't go here. If you do, the rules say you must add a penalty stroke and replay the shot from the same spot.

Through the green. The entire golf hole you are currently playing, from tee to green. Not, as it is mistakenly referred to, a ball that goes over, or past, the putting green.

1
PUTTING

Let's get right down to business. I have chosen to cover putting (and the rest of the short game) first, because I want to impress upon you the importance of learning to score. Putting can make or break you; you can save a lot of strokes over the course of a round if you are good with a putter. Likewise, you can ruin an otherwise good round with just a few bad putts.

Half of the strokes you use in a round of golf are with the putter, so you have to accept the fact that you will need to practice your putting (and the rest of the short game) at least as much as you practice your full swing. Another good reason to start with putting is because it is the simplest motion in golf, and mastering this technique will help you learn the other techniques required by golf much faster. As well, you will be making putts immediately as you do the drills I give you, and hopefully you will begin to feel that golf is not so hard after all.

Although there have been great putters who use a lot of wrist, and great putters who use almost no wrist, I teach putting without wrist action because it is a simpler, more controllable motion. You will be able to control both your distance and your club face alignment more easily with a wristless stroke. With that said, it is entirely up to you to decide how you putt best. However you choose to swing the putter, the drills in this chapter will make you a better putter, so practice them religiously.

The Putting Hold

There are just two important notes on how to hold the putter, otherwise it is a matter of personal preference. The **grip** is a part of the club. You **hold** the club; that's why I call it the putting hold, rather than the putting grip.

1. Thumbs go straight down the top of the shaft. Hold the putter with its sole flat on the ground. You will be looking down at what we will call the "top" of the shaft. Most putter grips have a flat side which is on the top of the shaft. Your thumbs should point straight down the flat side. You can lock your fingers together or overlap them in any way that feels comfortable.

2. Palms face each other. Try to align the grip along the lifeline of both palms. Your palms should face each other so that the backs of your hands are parallel.

Here are some of the most common putting grips. Give each a shot and see what works best for you.

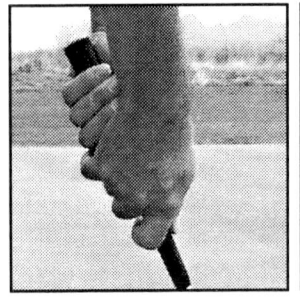

Overlap
The overlap hold is commonly used for the full swing, but you can use it for putting as well. All you have to do is overlap your right hand little finger atop your left index finger.

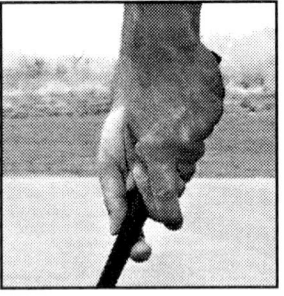

Reverse Overlap
The reverse overlap is very popular with golfers of all levels. Different from the Overlap grip, in the Reverse Overlap the left index finger overlaps the right little finger, although you may feel free to overlap more of your right hand if it feels more comfortable.

Cross Hand
The cross hand hold is gaining popularity among golfers for the following reasons: your shoulders are more level to the ground, which makes your stroke more level; the back of your left wrist is flat at address, which is where it should remain throughout the stroke; and because your right elbow will be closer to your body, encouraging a pendulum-like stroke. I urge you to give this hold a try. It really works for many people.

Right Hand Controls
Note the way the club rests in my right hand. It's very much in the palm. Your putting hold needs to be comfortable more than anything. You have to feel like you are going to make putts with it.

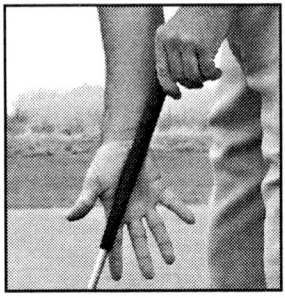

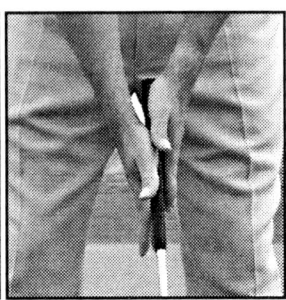

Parallel Hands
Look at the back of both hands, they are very nearly parallel. The most important thing to remember is that whatever your wrists do, the club head will also do, so keep your wrist movement to a minimum.

PUTTING SETUP

I don't want this to sound overly simple but, well, it really is simple. All you have to do is set your body, particularly your shoulders, parallel to the target line, place the ball two inches left of the center of your stance, and make sure your eyes are directly above the ball. Once you find your most comfortable posture that allows your eyes to be over the ball, you may find that you have to choke down on your putter. You can also have it cut down so that you don't have to choke down. Considering that the more you bend from the hip joints, the straighter you can swing the putter both back and forward, you may need a putter that's quite a bit shorter than you can buy off the rack. Fit the putter to your setup, not your setup to the putter. I find that almost all of my students need their putter cut down to fit them.

THE BALL DROP DRILL
You will putt more accurately if your eyes are over the target line. While set up to a ball, drop another ball from the bridge of your nose to check the position of your eyes. The ball you drop should land on top of the ball you have set up to.

TOO FAR FROM THE BALL
Eyes inside the ball won't accurately see the line to the hole.

RIGHT ON THE MARK
Eyes over the ball see the line much more accurately.

POOR POSTURE
Compare the angle of my back in this picture to the picture on the right. Standing too straight will cause my stroke to travel in more of an arc as it moves back and forward, rather than in a straight line, which can make consistency a problem. As well, my eyes are not over the ball.

GOOD POSTURE
How much you bend from the waist is a matter of preference. You can bend more than this or less, but make certain that your eyes are over the ball.

The Iron Triangle

The **Iron Triangle** is one of the most important concepts you will learn from this book. It is the foundation of your entire golf game. You will use the Iron Triangle in every shot you play. This concept, once mastered, will help you gain accuracy in the short game, and both power and accuracy in the long game.

Put a club down on the ground and align your **stance line** (the line across the tips of your toes) parallel to the club shaft. Stand with your feet about six inches apart, legs slightly flexed. You will not have a club in your hands yet.

Now bend from the waist a comfortable amount and let your arms hang freely, straight down to the ground. If your hands are touching your legs, you need to bend more from the waist. Straighten your arms and press the palms of your hands together. Your arms form the **Iron Triangle**, which I will often refer to as the **Triangle**.

Now simply move your Triangle slowly back and forth without bending your elbows or wrists. Watch your hands and arms while you swing back and forth. Notice how your shoulders will have to control the movement in order to keep your Triangle intact.

Watch how your hands move while you move your Triangle. Notice that if you stand more erect, your hands move in an arc, and that as you bend over more, your hands move in a straighter line. Try bending over from the waist more or less to find the right amount of bend which allows you to effortlessly move your hands in a straight line back and forth.

- Make sure that you do not bend your arms or wrists, and try to keep your knees as still as possible.

- Try to feel that your shoulders are rocking up and down like a seesaw to move the Triangle.

The manner in which you are standing is called your **putting posture**, and I've been a little vague on purpose. I want you to assume a posture which feels comfortable to *you*. Some people will bend more than others, and some will stand very straight. There is no *right* way to do it, and that's just fine.

DRILL

THE IRON TRIANGLE PUTT

Holding the putter as shown before, straighten your arms to form the **Iron Triangle**. Without hitting a ball, swing your Triangle back and forth in a pendulum-like motion. For starters, I'd like the length of swing to be about a foot back from, and forward of, your starting (address) position.

As you swing, watch your hands and arms, *not your putter*. You are trying to keep your arms and wrists from bending at all. Keep your knees, legs and hips as still as possible. **Do not hit a ball yet, just make certain that your technique is correct!**

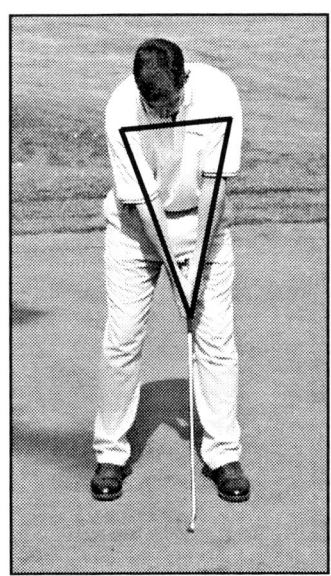

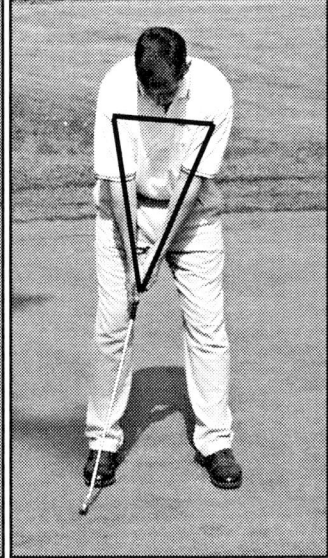

THE IRON TRIANGLE

No breakdown in the wrists or elbows throughout the motion. Basically, the only moving parts are your hands, arms, and shoulders. Before you try this with a ball, make several swings watching your Triangle move. Keep it intact as you push back and forward. Also monitor your legs. Make sure that they remain very still as you swing.

DRILL

THE PUSH

Many beginning and intermediate golfers suffer through putting problems that stem from using too big of a backswing. The result is an inevitable deceleration through impact. All distance control is lost with such a stroke. The Push drill will help you avoid this problem.

SETUP

- Set your feet a comfortable distance apart.
- Position the ball two inches left of the center of your stance.
- Place your putter head directly behind the ball.
- Position your hands slightly in front of the putter head.

THE DRILL

Push the ball into the hole, keeping your Triangle intact and the putter face aimed toward the hole all the while. Hold your finish and check to see that you did not break your Triangle, nor change the putter face aim. Adjust your finish if need be.

LESS IS BETTER

Some people prefer to have their arms and wrists bent at address for putting. If doing so feels more comfortable to you, feel free to. The important thing is that you do not change the amount of bend during the stroke. Extra movement can cause inconsistency in both putter face alignment and distance control.

DRILL

THE PUTTING TRACK

Lay down two clubs (2x4's work great, too) parallel to each other. Leave enough room between them to fit your putter head, with one-half inch extra room on both sides. The shafts create a putting track that will help you learn to make a **square** stroke, back and forward along the target line. Center a ball between the clubs, and push the ball again.

Once it becomes easy to push the ball through the track without hitting either side, begin using a short backswing and forward push to stroke putts. Begin with a backswing of about four inches with an equal length or slightly longer follow through. If you find this drill very difficult, that means you are not ready for the ball yet. Just practice your stroke without the distraction of the golf ball until you own your stroke.

Be sure to watch the ball, not the putter, as you putt.

Don't bother to look at where the ball goes when you hit it. You are working on your stroke at this time, not trying to get the ball into the hole. If fact, you shouldn't be near a hole when you do this drill. It is vital that you have no target in mind when practicing your mechanics. Remember that!

As you get more proficient with the track drill, place the shafts (or 2x4's) closer together. If you can get them to a tolerance of one-eighth of an inch, you are just plain awesome.

ON TRACK
The benefit of a straight back and forward putting stroke is that there is much less chance for timing errors. If the putter is always square to the target line, you can't miss. No, it is not necessary that you have a perfect stroke, but it sure can't hurt.

Distance control:
Control how far you hit the ball by adjusting the length of backswing you take. Use the shortest backswing possible that will allow you to get the ball one foot past the hole without causing you to lose the smoothness and rhythm of your stroke. Smoothly accelerate through impactm without becoming jerky or wristy, and you will be well on your way to great putting.

There is another factor that influences the direction and distance of your putts. You already know that the putter face must be aimed square to your target at impact for the ball to go there; that your stroke should be quite straight back and forward; and that you will control your distance by using shorter or longer strokes. However, you must also contact the ball on the sweetspot of the putter, otherwise, the putter will twist at impact, sending the ball off line and shorter than it would otherwise have gone.

To check where your putter's sweetspot is, hold the club up in one hand, and tap the face with the side of a coin until you find the spot where the club does not twist when you tap it. That's the sweetspot. It's not very big, is it? Using a magic marker, mark the top of the putter, even with the sweetspot, so that when you look down at the putter at address, the sweetspot's location is in clear view. Try to hit the ball with the sweetspot. Place some kind of tape or baby powder on the face so that impact will leave an impression, and you will know for certain whether you are hitting the sweet spot.

OK, one last thing: When you putt for real, make sure you do not work on your stroke. You must turn off your mechanical mind and focus on the target. You'll hear that again, because it is essential to playing good golf.

TARGET LOCK

As you take your last look at the target, say and do the "Target Lock." The idea is to lock the target in mind with your last look, slowly move your eyes back to the ball, and then after a brief pause, start the motion while still seeing the target in your mind's eye. I have my students say "Target Lock" out loud just to remind themselves to do it. Lock onto a very small target like a blade of grass on the putting green, or a small spot in the fairway to allow your mind focus with precision. Target Lock every shot you hit. It pays off.

Chapter 1   Putting 25

The Grind

Let me tell you about something I call THE GRIND. The Grind refers to the break-in period all golfers have to go through in order to *correctly* learn the skills required to play good golf. It takes strong commitment and perseverance to get through this period, and I am sad to say that many golfers never do make it. They expect golf to come naturally and it just doesn't. Whether you are working on your putting touch or your full swing, you will have to grind for a while. Make sure that you practice correctly so that you learn what you intend to learn. Grinding pays off, but only when you are ready. And you are not ready until you *own* your new skills. Don't give up. You weren't very good at tying your shoes when you first learned how, were you?

Watch Out for These Mistakes

Wrist Breakdown
You'll lose distance control, and make it unnecessarily difficult to keep your putter face aimed at the hole during your stroke.

Body Rotation
You need to keep your legs and hips very still during your putting stroke, otherwise you will force the stroke off line.

Stopping at Impact
Your follow through should be longer than your backswing. Take only as much backswing as you need, and accelerate through the ball, to the target.

Congratulations!

When you feel confident about the quality of your stroke, congratulate yourself on a job well done and realize that you are pretty much finished with the mechanics of putting. You should review your mechanics periodically, just to fine tune and maintain your good technique. But from now on, you should spend far more of your time doing the following drills, concentrating on the target only, without mechanics on your mind at all. Before you go on, however, you *really* need to know about the Pre-Shot Routine.

The Pre-Shot Routine, Part 1

Do you *really* want to get good? Then do this:

Before every putt, stand behind the ball, face the hole, and imagine the path the ball will take on its way into the hole. "See" the ball go into the hole, and "hear" the sound it will make as it clanks to a rest in the hole. Imagination is very important in golf.

Then take two or more rehearsal strokes while looking at the hole. *Rehearse* exactly what you intend to do (note: you may stand to the side of the ball rather than behind it, if it feels more comfortable). Don't *practice* your mechanics. Try to feel the stroke required to make the ball roll the proper distance. While you make these "feel it" rehearsal strokes, again imagine the ball rolling into the hole. You are creating a connection between yourself and the target, not practicing your stroke. The more clearly you can "see it" and "feel it," the better your connection will be. Get this point straight: Practice strokes are for working on your mechanics. Rehearsal strokes are for making putts.

While still standing behind the ball, (you have not yet addressed the ball) pick out a very small target such as a blade of grass that the ball will roll over on its way to the hole, and lock that target in your mind. Try to see a two-inch wide line from your ball to your target.

Step up to the ball and **aim your putter**. Next, **align yourself** (take your stance) to the putter. Then, run your eyes back and forth, along your line. Do this "tracking" with your eyes slowly, and try not to let your eyes "jump" along the line (that will take some practice). Then, when your brain tells you that you are ready, **putt the ball**. If it goes in, go take it out of the hole. If not, hit it again.

This is only a small introduction to the Pre-Shot Routine, but it is absolutely imperative that you use your routine if you want to give yourself the best possible chance for success. You must have only the target in mind when you are practicing *making* putts. Technical thoughts will only interfere with your awareness of the target, and since the object is to get the ball to the target...

In sum, your Pre-Shot Routine should consist of three steps to program yourself for success:

1 **See it**. Visualize. See the shot as you want it to happen.

2 **Feel it**. Feel the distance, not the mechanics.

3 **Do it**. Target Lock and go.

CHAPTER 1   PUTTING   27

Following are a bunch of putting drills which you would do well to permanently include in your practice routine. I realize that you probably have a job, maybe even kids, and that practice time is limited. However, if you skip putting practice, the score card will know it!

As you continue learning with this book, you are going to get a lot of mechanical ideas running through your head. Let me tell you, it's *hard* to let go of those mechanical thoughts and just concentrate on the target. Your ability to focus on the target will constantly be put to the test in golf. You are going have to practice that skill, just like you practice any other part of your game. It is precisely this sort of practice that enables good players to bring to the course, the same game they had on the range.

USE YOUR ROUTINE!

I'm not sure if funny is the right word, but it's funny how many times I have to remind students to go through their routine every time they have a target in mind. I guess some people feel like they're wasting valuable time on something unimportant. Listen to me now, and hear me later: You have to practice getting your brain in gear to hit your best shots, and it's too late if you wait 'till you get to the course to practice that.

DRILL

THE ONE FOOTER

Find a straight, slightly uphill, one foot putt. It is most important to have a straight putt for this drill.

Place the ball one foot from the hole (target). Go through your pre-shot routine, and putt the ball. This drill will teach you to aim your putter face to the target, and to keep your putter head square to (facing) the target through impact.

Hold your followthrough and make sure that your putter face is still square.

After you get real good at this drill, increase the distance to two and then three feet. Twenty-five in a row from three feet is fantastic! For the really ambitious, try four and five footers, too.

I know one foot seems like an awfully short distance, but putting is all about confidence. You gain confidence by making lots of putts. You lose confidence by missing lots of putts. Don't practice missing. You might get good at it.

Another great drill is to practice putting to a small coin on the green (or the floor) as your target. Do this drill enough, and the hole will look like a basketball hoop.

ABOUT PRACTICING

It is very important to have a goal and a consequence in your practice. For example, having to start all over again can heighten your intensity, which will make your practice even more effective. Give yourself a specified amount of time to complete each drill and/or a certain number of putts you have to make, and force yourself to stay there until you reach your number, or run out of time.

DRILL

AIMING EXERCISE

Aiming the putter face well is the most difficult part of making those short putts. This drill will show you exactly what a square putter face looks like and will train you to see the "line" to the hole. You can also use the tape to train your stroke.

On a level floor (short carpet works great) lay a piece of electrical tape in a straight line, fifteen feet long. The tape serves as your line to the hole. A great idea is to put a small mirror over the line at one end, so that you can check that your eyes are over the line at address.

In address position, place your putter face perpendicular to the line and take a good look at it. That's what perfect alignment looks like. Moving only your head, look at the far end of the line, and then back to your putter face. Run your eyes back and forth along the line and absorb what perfect aim is. A well aimed putter may look strange at first. No problem. The more often you do this drill, the more familiar perfect alignment will look to you.

As a separate drill, make some strokes over the line. This will help train your stroke. And as another drill, try a few putts and see if you can keep the ball on the line. Start with short putts (two feet) and progress to the full length of the line. If the floor is not level, DO NOT PUTT ANY BALLS. You'll do more damage to your stroke than good.

Reading Greens

The science (art?) of green reading is learned through experience. It takes considerable time on the greens to learn how varying degrees of slope will affect the roll of the ball. To read a green properly, you must consider whether your putt will move uphill or downhill, break to the right or left, be into the grain or with the grain, or be affected by wind. Let me help you assess these variables.

To read putts, get at least ten feet behind the ball and squat down. You may want to walk to the opposite side of the hole and do the same thing. While you walk to the other side, keep looking around the hole. Circle around the hole to the other side as you return to your ball to get a view from all sides for the best read. As you walk around, be aware of your feet. They, too, can help you feel the slope.

If, through surveying the area around your ball and the hole, you determine that the putt is downhill, meaning you are standing above the hole, you must keep in mind that the ball will roll farther than a flat putt. You will need to hit the putt more softly than a flat putt of the same distance. You may want to imagine that the hole is closer to you than it really is. In addition, since you are hitting the ball more softly, it will break (curve) more than a more level or uphill, breaking putt, as it slows down. You will have to allow for more break on downhill putts.

When the ball is below the hole (you are putting uphill), you can afford to be more aggressive with your stroke. Definitely hit these putts hard enough to hit the back of the cup. Since you will hit the ball a little harder, it will stay on line better for you, so you can play a straighter line to the hole. Note that if you hit the ball too slowly on an uphill, breaking putt, the ball will break hard as it slows down. You may want to imagine that the hole is farther from you than it really is.

On breaking putts, you have to guess how much they will curve. Obviously, the more experience you have, the better your guess will be. After you determine how much the ball will curve, aim your putter not to the hole, but to a spot far enough to the side of the hole to allow the ball to break into the hole. For example, if I read six inches of break from left to right, I will pick a spot (a blade of grass works well) six inches left of the hole and aim the putter there. I make that spot my target, and try to putt the ball there.

The most important thing you can do is hit a lot of putts and see for yourself what happens. Go through your pre-shot routine each time, including reading the green. The more putts you read, hit, and evaluate the feedback from, the better you will become at reading greens.

> Most amateurs fail to play enough break when putting. Always give the ball a chance to roll into the "high side" of the hole and you will make more putts. (If the putt breaks right to left, the right side of the hole is the high side). A good idea is to double the amount of break you read, pick your spot, and putt to your spot.

Southern golf courses usually have Bermuda grass on their greens during the warm months, and then overseed with another strain of grass such as Bluegrass for the winter months. Especially when playing on Bermuda greens, you must take note of what is called "grain." Grain refers to the direction in which the grass grows on the green. Grass grows toward water, or bends away from prevailing winds, and can significantly influence the roll of the ball.

Basically speaking, if the grass is shiny along the path to the hole, you are putting with the grain and the effect will be a faster putt. The opposite is true if the grass is dull, indicating that you are against the grain. When you are against the grain, the break will be more severe and the ball will stop sooner than normal. You need to hit putts firmly when putting against the grain. If you are putting a level putt, but the grain is going to the right (or left), the putt will break right (or left), eventhough it looks dead straight. Grain will have some effect on all greens, although much more so on Bermuda, so take grain into account when reading all putts.

Practice Your Putting

When most people practice, they completely ignore putting. They go straight to the range and hit drivers until they are too tired or frustrated to swing, and then they go home and sulk. Remember this, you can often make up for a poorly hit drive or approach shot, but when you miss a putt, the shot is lost forever. Include putting at every practice session if you want to shoot lower scores.

One more thing. Change the width of your stance to find out whether you putt better with your feet close or far apart. Do your drills with your feet close, and then do them again with them wider. A little experimentation could really make a difference!

DRILL

THREE BALL

For this distance control drill, take three balls and place them side by side, six inches apart, at a start distance of about ten feet from the hole.

Visualize the shot. Feel the right stroke. Step up to the ball. Aim your putter. Align yourself. Target Lock. And when your brain says you're ready, putt. Watch where the ball goes and adjust appropriately. If the last putt was too short, hit the next one farther, and vice versa. Go through your routine with each ball, and adjust each ball to the desired distance. If the last putt went in, do it again!

Do not evaluate how well you do this drill, there are no bad shots, only adjustments to be made. Simply let your mind soak up the information. Just think "that was neat, let's try this."

Do this drill from every distance you can find, uphill, downhill, and sidehill, and you will quickly improve your distance control.

The idea of this drill is to give yourself more and more experience to rely upon for future putts. Read and stroke the first putt, and closely watch the ball roll to learn how accurate your read was. Then reread the next putt, now having a better idea of what the ball will do, thinking "so that's what that amount of break looks like." Do it once again for your third putt.

DISTANCE CONTROL

You definitely want to give yourself a chance to make the putt, but you don't want the ball cruising four or five feet past the hole. Attempt to get the ball just one foot past the hole, and you'll always be left with a tap-in, which is good for the blood pressure.

DRILL

TWELVE BALL

Starting ten feet from the target, place twelve balls in a straight line, three feet apart. Go through your pre-shot routine and start from the ball closest to the hole. **See it**, **Feel it**, and **Do it**. Then **Review it** if necessary. If the ball did not either go in, or about one foot past the hole, take a couple more practice strokes trying to feel the right one. Review strokes will help you learn just as much as your practice strokes and your actual putt.

Move on through all twelve balls with the same attention to your pre-shot routine, and please, for your sake, read every putt.

SPEED IS THE KEY
Distance putts are all about speed. How hard you hit the ball will not only affect how far the ball goes, it will also affect how much a putt will break.

DRILL

AROUND THE WORLD

By now, you are ready for an advanced putting drill which will help you with short, breaking putts. Place twelve balls in a circle around the hole, all two feet from the hole. Use a hole with some slope to it so that you can practice breaking putts. Go through your **pre-shot routine** (have you heard that before?), and putt the first ball. If you make it, take the ball out of the hole, put it aside, and go on to the next ball. If you miss it, replace it, and go on to the next ball. When you have gone through the circle of balls, go back to those you replaced and make five in a row from each spot. Around the World is a great short putting drill which will really help you lower your score. Try to do it with three and four footers as well.

DRILL

NORTH, SOUTH, EAST, AND WEST

Make four piles of five balls, and place them to the North, South, East, and West of the hole, three paces away (that's just about ten feet). Mark each spot with a tee or a coin. You must make three out of the five in order to go to the next pile. Again, you should use a hole with some break to it. Oh, make sure you use your routine. Have I said that enough yet?

Sometimes, these drills will take more time than you would really like. All I can say is, stick with them. They will lead directly to lower scores.

IT'S ALL CONFIDENCE
You can become a really good putter if you put your time in. Practice making lots of putts, and you'll think of yourself as a good putter. That's confidence.

DRILL

THE TWENTY FOOTER

Take three balls and place them seven paces from the hole (that's about twenty feet). Mark the spot with a tee. Take three more balls and place them on the opposite side of the hole at the same distance. Go through your routine each time, and try to putt the ball into the hole. If you get all three balls within a putter's length of the hole, you get one point. Go to the other side and do the same. Your goal is to get to four points. The catch is that if any ball is not within a putter's length, you must start the drill over again from zero.

I'll tell you what, if you run through these drills every time you make it to the practice green, you can't help but get good. You can and will improve quickly if you put in the time and concentration. You just have to decide that you want to get good, and then commit to practicing regularly and for an extended period. Don't expect to be a scratch golfer after six months. That's crazy. You know what? Don't *expect* anything. Just practice because you enjoy it, and know you are on the path to good golf. You'll improve faster, having relieved yourself of the pressure your expectations put on you.

I certainly realize that the drills I have given you may make practice more like work. Here are a couple of games you can play with friends to make practice more fun *and* get a little pressure involved so you get used to making putts when it counts. Play for a little something to make it interesting.

Draw back

Draw back is a touch improving game for you to play with one or more players. In draw back, the idea is to putt the ball to within one club length of the hole, but not short of the hole. If your ball ends up short of the hole, or more than one club length past or to the side of the hole, you must then draw the ball back an additional club length and then try to make it from there. Keep putting and drawing back as necessary until you get the ball into the hole.

These putts may be of any length. Practice relatively short putts (as close as 10 feet) as well as some long bombs and breaking putts. Play a specified amount of holes keeping track of total score, and you will become a better putter under pressure, while having fun practicing. You can't beat that with a stick!

21

With a friend, play closest to the hole from varying distances. You don't have to play the hole out. Here's how to keep score. Closest to the hole gets 1 point. Making the putt is worth 3 points. And if you make a putt after the other player has made it, you get 6 points and the other person gets 3. The first person to reach 21 points exactly, wins. You have to get 21 exactly. If you go over 21, then you go back to 15 and continue the game from there.

Two Putt

Play a specified number of holes (nine is good) and keep track of how many strokes you take for each hole. Par for each hole is 2, so you want to use 18 or fewer putts for the nine holes you play. One variation on this game is to continue playing sets of nine holes until you do use 18 or fewer putts. Another variation is to play the first nine, and then try to better your score on the second nine. If you don't better your score, you have to play nine more holes. A third variation is to play against someone else, and try to beat their score.

2
CHIPPING

We're going to move a little farther from the hole, to just off of the green. As we continue through the book, we will progress farther from the green until a full swing is required to get the ball to the hole.

The short game; putting, chipping and pitching, accounts for about 65% of the strokes all golfers use in a round of golf. **65%!!!** You owe it to yourself to have a really good short game. You may never hit a 300 yard drive like some of the tour pros, but you can have almost as good a short game. It's just a matter of a little technique and a lot of quality practice time.

Before we get into the actual chip, however, there are some things we have to get straight.

The Full Swing Hold

I have included the full swing hold here because you must have it to chip the ball well. Although you can afford to be more of an individualist with the putting hold, as we move onto chipping, pitching, and the full swing, you will need a fundamentally sound hold that will help you deliver the club squarely to the ball, with the least amount of effort. A square club face aims straight to the target. If you hold the club improperly, you will have difficulty getting the club face square at impact. There are several points to learn about the hold, and they are all important. Practice your hold until it's automatic.

Chapter 2 — Chipping 41

Left Hand

With your right hand, hold the club shaft (just below the grip) just about perpendicular to the ground. Your right hand should be chest high. The bottom (or leading) edge of the club face should point straight toward the sky. With the club like this, you will be looking at the "top" of the club. Visualizing a clock face, refer to the top as the "Twelve O'clock" position.

1. Move your left hand, fingers extended, to the side of the grip until you can put your fingers around it. When you take hold of the grip, your fingers should be just about perpendicular to the club shaft.

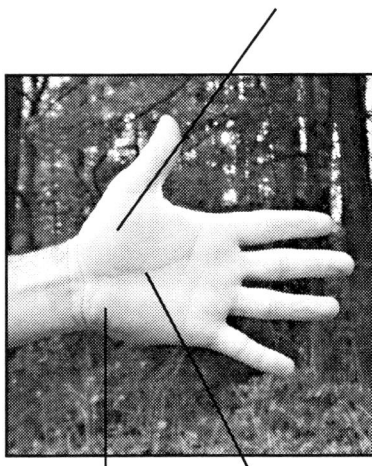

Thumb Pad

2. The heel pad, as opposed to the thumb pad, should rest on top of the club, lending support to your hold. Your little finger and ring finger will do most of the work holding the club.

Heel Pad   Life Line

3. You should see the first (big) knuckles of your index and middle fingers, possibly that of your ring finger too. The "V" formed by the index finger and thumb points to your right shoulder. Your left thumb should sit slightly to the right of the top, at the One O'clock position.

Heel Pad on Top

Be sure to look straight down when you check your knuckles. Don't tilt your head to the side. Your view won't be accurate.

RIGHT HAND

While holding the club in your left hand (with your new hold of course) here's how to place your right hand on the club.

1. Place your right hand so that the club rests mainly in the fingers. Although, in the end, all your fingers will be on the grip, your middle two fingers will do most of the holding.

2. The right side of your left thumb should rest in the lifeline (the line between the heel pad and thumb pad) of your right hand. Your palms should face each other.

3. Your right thumb will sit slightly to the left of the top, at the 11 o'clock position; its "V" pointing to your right shoulder.

4. Use one of three ways to join your hands.

The Overlap
Place the little finger of your right hand over your left index finger, or between the index and middle fingers. This is the most common hold for men and stronger women.

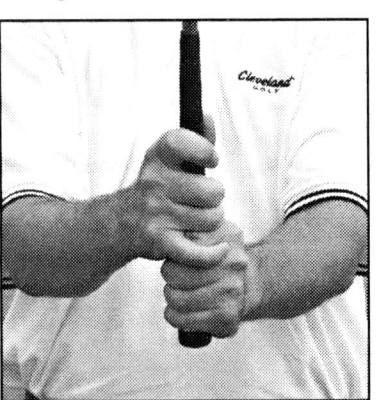

The Interlock
Lock your hands together by inserting your right little finger between the left index and middle fingers. Use this hold if you have short fingers.

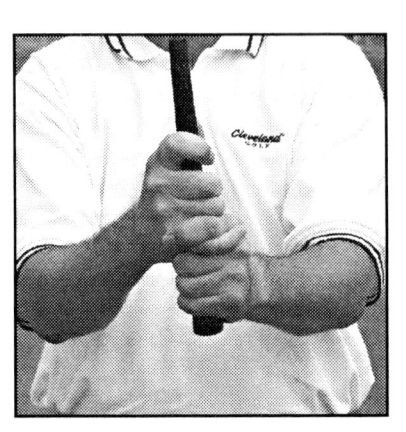

The Ten-finger
Bring your hands together so that the right little finger rests against the left index finger. This is a great hold for all beginners and children.

CHAPTER 2   CHIPPING 43

Here are a few checkpoints to remember about your hold:

- Your hands should fit snugly together and share control over the club. Your palms should be parallel to each other.

- You will have two "V's" formed by the crease between the thumb and index finger of each hand. These V's should point to your right shoulder. You should see two or three knuckles of your left hand.

- Keep a constant eye on your hold. It will want to change on you at first, so make sure you review the keys.

Now let's practice holding the club to ingrain the proper hold. Take your hands off the club and start all over again as before. When you are sitting in front of the TV, mindlessly watching something, practice holding the club. At least you'll be less likely to become hypnotized. When that becomes easy, and feels comfortable, rest the club head on the ground in front of you, and practice your hold.

Don't take your hold lightly (like that pun?). The hold is the first fundamental of golf. Before you ever attempt to swing the club, be automatic with your hold.

A COUPLE OF NOT-SO-HOT HOLDS

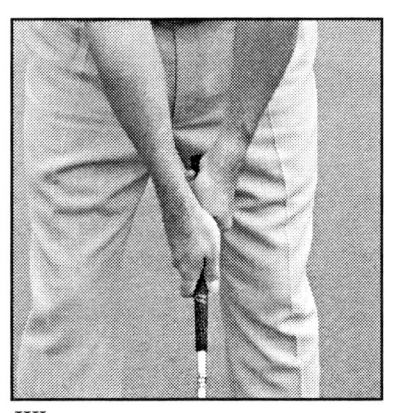

WEAK
My left thumb is directly on top of the grip, and my right hand is too far over to my left. This is an "open face" hold, and will cause the ball to curve to the right.

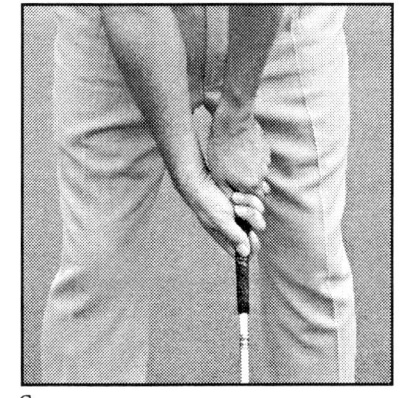

STRONG
My V's are over to far, pointing outside my right shoulder, and I can see four knuckles of my left hand. This is a "closed face" hold, and will cause the ball to curve to the left.

CHIPPING SETUP

A chip is a lot like a putt with a hop in it. The setup is the only major difference, and will take just a little time to get comfortable with. Use a sand wedge or pitching wedge at first, then try using other clubs.

Stand about six inches from the ball, and position yourself so that the ball is even with the outside of your right heel. This may seem uncomfortably close at first, but trust me, it will become natural with a little practice. Your feet should be quite close together, about two or three inches between your heels is good. Shift your weight so that it is mainly on your left foot, but not so much that you are off balance. Try to get your shoulders parallel to the ground.

To help you swing the club along the target line, your stance line should be slightly to the left of the target line. This is called an **open stance**, as opposed to a **square** (parallel to the target line) **stance**.

Now place your club right behind the ball, resting lightly on the ground. Don't push the club down into the ground, because you may make the ball move, which is a penalty. Many good players hold the club slightly above the ground to avoid snagging the club in the grass on the backswing.

With your stance line left and your weight left, point your club shaft as nearly perpendicular to the ground as possible without forcing your hold to change. Push your hands forward, toward the target, until they are ahead of (closer to the target) the ball and the back of your left wrist is flat. This **forward press** will set your hands exactly where you'll what them to be at impact. Be careful that you don't let the club face turn as you push your hands forward. With your setup complete, *get the ball out of the way before you attempt to learn the stroke!*.

Recall your **Iron Triangle** putting stroke. Without breaking your wrists or elbows, bring your Triangle back and through, as straight along the target line possible. To help learn the idea of a straight back and through swing, you may want to practice your chipping stroke in the same manner as the Putting Track drill, (two clubs on the ground side by side). By the way, the chip and the putt are the only shots that use a straight back and forward stroke.

CHAPTER 2   CHIPPING 45

For now, forget about any target at all. Forget about the ball even. You need to be free to concentrate solely on your technique. Get the technique down first, and introduce the ball only after you are satisfied with your stroke. Then work on contact and accuracy using your good technique. It takes very little time to learn correctly, but far longer to correct a bad habit.

CHIPPING KEYS:

The setup is very important. A good setup makes it easier to contact the ball solidly. That's the reason for such a detailed description. It may seem a little uncomfortable, but it works.

1. **Stand about six inches from the ball and position the ball even with the outside of your right heel.**
2. **Align your stance slightly left of the target.**
3. **Put your weight on your left foot.**
4. **Push your hands forward, ahead of the ball until the back of your left wrist is flat.**
5. **Swing the Iron Triangle back and through (your backswing and forward swing should be just about equal in length).**

SETUP FOR SUCCESS

Weight left, stance aligned left, hands well in front of the ball. The set up may feel strange at first, but it makes solid contact much easier to achieve.

DRILL

THE IRON TRIANGLE CHIP

Set up as described. Take note of the position of your hands and wrists at address. Make an **Iron Triangle** backswing of about eighteen inches from the ball and stop. Check to see if your wrists have bent. If they have, start again. Try to remove as much wrist action as possible, but avoid being rigid, or "death gripping" the club. A little looseness in your hands is good for touch.

Now swing forward through impact, toward the target. Hold your finish position and check your wrists and arms. *NO BENDING!!!* Make sure that you check both backswing and followthrough. Don't break the Iron Triangle! Note: Your followthrough should now be a little longer than your backswing.

CHAPTER 2   CHIPPING 47

DRILL

THE LONG CLUB

The Long Club is a tool I use to help my students learn the proper chipping technique. It works magic for students who have trouble breaking their wrists during the stroke. I have cut a hole in the butt of my pitching wedge and inserted an old shaft so that about two or three feet of the old shaft protrudes from the butt of the wedge. Take your normal hold on the wedge, and let the extra length of shaft rest against your body, under your left arm. Don't rest the shaft against your arm, however.

Practice chipping as usual, but don't let the shaft come off of your body at any time during the stroke. If you get wristy with your backswing, the shaft will leave your side.

THE IRON TRIANGLE; A GOLFER'S BEST FRIEND

Just as in putting, the Iron Triangle image will greatly help you learn. The Long Club makes it easy to learn the perfect motion. You can also use The Long Club for shorter pitch shots, covered in Chapter 3.

DRILL

Downward Contact

Keep in mind that you must try to hit the ball as your club is moving downward, toward the ground. A descending hit will get the ball in the air for you. You need not help the ball up by lifting or scooping it. You may want to make several practice swings where you take your backswing and then simply hit down into the grass until your club cuts through the grass and hits the ground. Here's a neat way to make sure you are hitting down properly.

Setup as normal, but place another ball about eight inches behind the original ball. Chip the ball you've setup to, making sure you avoid the one behind. If you do not descend sharply enough, you will hit the wrong ball. Instant feedback. I love that!

Weight Stays Left

Keeping your weight on your left foot throughout the chipping stroke will help you make good contact, which is the key to these short shots. Try lifting your right heel off the ground a couple of inches and keep it there through the shot. Your weight will have to stay left, just as it should.

DRILL

Pick a Spot

After you get your technique down, it's time to move on and try to make your chips go in the hole. You should monitor your technique from time to time, but the point of learning the correct technique is to forget it and just hit the shot.

Get a small towel or handkerchief and place it on the ground or the putting green as a target. Using a sand wedge, try to chip balls onto your target. Get used to the idea of picking out a spot onto which you will land your chips. You can do this drill at the putting green, or in the backyard. All that's left is to learn how far the ball will roll, and that's easy. Get to a putting green where they allow chipping, and hit lots of chips and watch what happens.

Soon you will need to get good at imagining how far you want the ball to fly and how much it will roll. As you take your practice swings, try to feel how big a stroke you need. Remember that the rehearsal strokes are for feel, not for mechanical correctness. Whenever there is a target, forget your mechanics and concentrate on the target.

Try different clubs with the same target. Watch the difference in the way the ball rolls as you change from club to club. You need to try a lot of shots, from as many different positions as you can think of, to give yourself as much experience as you can. Experience is the key. If you are trying a shot for the first time, you may not be very good at it. But if you've practiced it before, you'll have a much better chance of success.

DRILL

UP AND DOWN

This drill introduces the idea of scoring. The idea of the drill is to chip the ball UP, close to the hole, and then putt it DOWN, into the hole. Two shots is the goal, but if you need more, go ahead, don't give up. This drill is what golf is all about, getting the ball into the hole in the fewest strokes possible. Set a goal for yourself. Don't end the drill until you have made a certain number of up and downs. Start with five and then increase your goal as you improve.

Note: Generally speaking, I like to have my students first develop good touch with the sand wedge and 9 Iron, and then introduce the other clubs later. For now, use the sand wedge (or pitching wedge, if that's what you have) for shorter shots (within about thirty feet of the hole), and 9 Iron for longer shots. A good guideline to follow is to fly the sand wedge one half the distance to the hole, letting the ball roll the remainder of the distance. Fly the 9 Iron about one third the distance to the hole. Land the ball on the green whenever possible; the ball will bounce straighter on the green.

As you advance, spend some time practicing with the sand wedge through the 6 Iron. You may find it easier to control your distance simply by using the same stroke and letting the differently lofted clubs send the ball farther or shorter. The more lofted clubs will roll the least, which is good for short chips, and the less lofted ones will give you the most roll, which can be used for longer chips.

Congratulations!

OK, if you can honestly say to yourself that your chipping technique is sound, and you don't have to think about it when you chip, congratulate yourself, and realize that you are done with the mechanics of chipping. You may need to review the mechanics periodically, but it is time to leave technical thoughts behind. You can now trust your technique, and focus your attention on the target. Become target oriented, not mechanics oriented. That's how you PLAY GOLF.

WATCH OUT FOR THESE MISTAKES

WRIST BREAKDOWN
Just as in putting, if your wrists break during the stroke, you invite a host of problems. Keep your Iron Triangle intact throughout the motion.

BALL POSITION TOO FORWARD
Positioning the ball too forward can make contact very difficult. Remember, the ball is positioned even with the outside of your right heel. In advanced golf, moving the ball forward helps you hit higher, softer chips. Try that later.

3
PITCHING

Moving right along... A pitch is a longer, higher version of a chip. Pitching includes the wide range of distances which require a longer swing than a chip, but a shorter than full swing. Let's just say, for our purposes, that a chip becomes a pitch when you have to carry the ball five yards or more in the air. The neat thing is that the same drills you do to learn pitching will also help you learn the full swing. We will start with address position, and then move onto the drills. I have found my students' progress to be nothing short of amazing by using these drills, and I suggest that you start every practice session with them. Use a sand wedge, or pitching wedge if you haven't got a sand wedge. You *really need* a sand wedge, however.

Address Position

Basically, address position refers to the way in which you stand to the ball. Address position is important because it *can* set you ready to make a good, balanced swing. Or not. Your posture, alignment, and ball position make up your address position. Here are the keys:

- **Stand straight with your feet directly under your shoulders and hold the club straight out in front of you.**
  Note: How far apart you set your feet will vary with club selection and the type of shot you are going to hit. Generally, play all *full* shots with the ball within two inches of the inside of your left heel. More on ball position later.

- **Flex your knees until you feel your thigh muscles just begin to work.**
  Similar to a baseball player's ready position in the outfield.

- **Push your behind out just a little, in order to keep your back straight and tilt your spine forward from your hip joints until the club hits the ground.**
  This should feel similar to the start of sitting down.

- **Let your arms hang straight down from your shoulder sockets.**
  Hang loose! Tension kills golf swings.

- **Tilt your spine slightly to the right.**
  Because your right hand is lower on the club than your left, your right shoulder is also lower than your left. Therefore, your spine tilts slightly to the right. Allow this tilt to occur. Don't try to level out your shoulders. Just let them relax.

- **Place your hands slightly in front of the club head.**

- **Place your weight about 70% on your heels (you should be able to wiggle your toes comfortably), and 60% on your right foot.**

At this time, check your balance and your tension level. You want to feel like you are set and ready for action, but loose. Somewhat like a baseball player out on the field. To check my students' address position, I will give them a little push backward and then forward. If they come off balance, we know they are a little off, requiring a change in either knee bend or waist bend. Watch out for your weight getting too far out over your toes. That's probably the most common error, and it sets you off balance right from the start.

Posture Check
Bend your knees just enough to feel your thigh muscles engage and allow your arms to hang naturally, straight down from your shoulders. A line drawn from the middle of your shoulder should fall on top of your toes.

ALIGNMENT is another part of address that is crucial for successful shotmaking. There are four components of alignment which you must check every time you set up to the ball. Lines across your **feet**, **thighs**, **shoulders**, and **forearms** should all be parallel to the target line. Always practice with a club on the ground to serve as an alignment aid, and you will go a long way toward getting the most out of your practice.

Solid Address
Perfect balance combined with feet, thighs, shoulders, and forearms aligned parallel to the target line.

That was an awful lot of talk about the address position, and it's important, but you don't ever need to think about it while swinging the club. Address position is a **pre-swing fundamental**. Once you set yourself properly, don't give it another thought. Obviously, setting yourself correctly will take time at first, but you will soon be able to do it without much thought at all. Keep in mind that when you address the ball, you can help yourself a lot by checking (and releasing) tension before you swing.

OK. We will start our pitching with a simple drill to teach you the real meaning of the "followthrough," called the **push**. Then we'll move onto an extension of the chipping motion called the **Half and Half Swing**, and finish off the longer pitches with the **Three Quarter and Half Swing**.

DO THESE DRILLS SLOWLY AND PERFECTLY!!!

Your improvement is directly related to the quality of your practice. Practice makes permanent. *Perfect* practice makes perfect. So practice perfectly and you will learn the right stuff. Fast. The following three drills should be done at the start of every practice session. As you first learn your swing, the drills will teach you the proper technique. They will also help you to maintain your swing throughout your career.

LISTEN. Eighty percent of the golfers in this country suffer from a disease called the slice. The slice is caused by a combination of the wrong club path and the wrong club face angle. Starting with this section, you will learn the proper mechanics (inside-out club path, and club face control) which will enable you to hit the ball with power and control if, and only if, you practice correctly. It is far more important to do fewer repetitions of *perfect* quality, than to do more repetitions of *almost* perfect quality. Impatience is your adversary. If you follow the instruction in this book, you will learn very quickly, but at your own pace. Be patient! Once again, DON'T INTRODUCE THE BALL UNTIL YOU ARE VERY COMFORTABLE WITH THE TECHNIQUE.

When you learn to ski, you don't jump on a double diamond run to start out, do you? The equivalent to doing that is to head to the golf course with a bunch of new ideas about how to swing the club, and try to practice your new moves during the round. Well, at least you can't get hurt on a golf course, but you won't learn anything either. If anything, you may *think* you are doing something different, but actually you're just making the same old mistakes. The conclusion you'll invariably come to is that the new stuff doesn't work, although you never actually did it right in the first place.

The key is to practice in the backyard or at the range slowly and with complete conscious control, so that you learn exactly what you are trying to learn. There are a lot of golfers out there who have taken the right instruction, only to go out and teach themselves something different. I strongly advise against that. There are also lots of golfers who have been given the wrong instruction and learned it perfectly. Well, all I can say is that, at least, this *is* the right instruction. Now it's up to you to teach yourself well. When I see a new student for the first time, I tell him/her, "Up to this point you may not have known how to practice well. I promise to teach you exactly what to practice and how, so from this point forward, if you practice wrong, it's your own fault." I'm just the coach. *You* are the teacher. Teach yourself correctly.

DRILL

THE PUSH

This is going to seem a little too easy, but please do The Push at the start of each practice session. No ball, please. Use your long club if you've made one.

The whole drill goes like this: Start at address and swing forward to what I call the Half Followthrough. Sounds simple, but you must learn to swing the club toward the target without breaking your Triangle, *and* allow your hips to rotate at the same time. Although your Triangle will lead your hips just slightly, your movement should be smooth and seamless.

Let me make it clear that the "followthrough" is different from the "finish." The **followthrough** is extension toward the target and occurs throughout the forward swing. The Half Followthrough ends when: the club shaft is nearly parallel to the ground and pointing toward the target; the Iron Triangle is still intact (no bending at the elbows or wrists); your hands are in front of your belly button; your belly button points to the target or to the left of it (if you can turn that far); your left leg is straight, holding virtually all of your weight on it; and your right shoulder is lower than your left. The **finish** is the final resting place of the full swing, and we are not doing that just yet. You own this drill when you come to the perfect Half Followthrough automatically.

STRAIGHT LINE DOWN THE FRONT OF THE BODY (SECOND PHOTO)
Note how straight the line from the front of my chest down my left leg is. No leaning.

Half Followthrough Keys:

- Belly button facing the target.
- Iron Triangle intact. Arms straight, wrists straight.
- Hands belly button high, club shaft points to the target.
- Left leg straight with almost all of your weight on it
- Right foot up on the toe, virtually weightless.
- Right shoulder lower than the left.

I think I need to explain why you should be so picky about this drill: For maximum power, you need to accelerate the club head all the way through impact, toward the target; In order to continue your acceleration through impact, your hips must rotate. If your hips don't rotate, you cannot possibly extend toward the target, and you will lose both power and control; If your wrists bend improperly, club face control becomes difficult, making consistency elusive; Your left leg supports your body weight on the forward swing. It must straighten as it receives your weight, or you will find it difficult to turn forward completely or make solid contact consistently; Finally, your spine angle must remain quite constant through impact to make good contact consistently. That means that if you stay in your posture (maintain your spine angle) as you turn on the backswing, your left shoulder will automatically be lower than your right (we haven't done the backswing yet), and as you followthrough, your right shoulder will be lower.

Hip Action
Train your body to properly rotate as the club pulls it around on the forward swing with The Push.

DRILL

THE HALF AND HALF SWING

All pitches require fundamentals you will learn from the Half and Half Swing, but that's not all this drill teaches you. The Half and Half Swing will also teach you to correctly start the backswing; to swing your Iron Triangle through impact; to rotate your hips properly through impact; to square the club face at impact; and to extend through impact. So not only will you learn short game techniques which you must *own* if you want to play good golf, you will also build a rock solid foundation for your full swing. You see, there *is* a madness to my method!

Start the Half Backswing by moving your Triangle back until the club shaft is parallel to the ground, parallel to the target line, and no higher than your belt. Then, smoothly accelerate the Triangle forward, through impact, until **your Triangle forces your hips to rotate** in order to continue the swing. Stop at the Half Followthrough, as you learned in The Push.

THE HALF BACKSWING

Check for the following: Triangle intact; club shaft parallel to the ground and the target line; weight solidly on flexed right leg. Most golfers ruin their swing in the first two or three feet of movement. Take care to get this drill right and you'll make golf easier.

Make sure that you maintain the flex in your right knee as you move the triangle backward, so that you feel your weight shift onto your right leg. Note that you should not have to force the weight shift. The motion of your arms, hips and shoulders, combined with a firmly flexed right knee should make the weight shift automatic.

Some movements that go on in your swing result from previous movement. The weight shift is one of them. Turn properly and your weight shifts, but don't *try* to shift your weight. While you move one part of your body, another part may move out of necessity. You must not try to avoid movement; you must train yourself to move what has to be moved and allow other movements to occur naturally.

Now, swing your Iron Triangle forward, toward the target, and allow your hips to rotate through impact. Stop at the Half Followthrough and check yourself.

Once again, the Long Club can really help with this drill. Don't let the shaft extension leave your side at any time during the swing.

THE TRIANGLE PULLS THE BODY AROUND

The Iron Triangle pulls the body through impact and on to the Half Followthrough. I'm extending my club, hands, and arms out to the target, just as though I were to toss a ball there underhanded.

Full Swing Address and Pitching Address

The only difference between the Half and Half Swing and a real pitch shot is how you address the ball. For a pitch, you will set your weight firmly on your left foot at address and keep it there throughout the shot, whereas in the drill, you start from full swing address. This also is true for the Three Quarter and Half Swing which follows.

Make certain that you understand the difference between **full swing address** (weight 60% on your right foot, right leg supports backswing), and **pitching address** (weight 90% on left foot, left leg supports entire swing).

FULL SWING ADDRESS   PITCHING ADDRESS

Ball Position
Note the difference in ball position (where the ball is relative to my feet). For all Full Swings, the ball is within two inches of the left heel, but for all pitch shots, the ball is near the right foot. For short pitches, as in the Half and Half, play the ball even with your right foot, as shown here. For longer pitches, move the ball just inside the right heel, as on page 65.

Pitching Address
My shoulders are more level and my weight is firmly on my left foot, where it will stay throughout the swing. My feet are very close together. Ball position is back toward my right foot, and I stand closer to the ball than for a full swing.

FULL SWING ADDRESS
Stance line (line across toes) is **square** (parallel) to the target line.

PITCHING ADDRESS
Stance line is **open** (to the left of the target line).

Do not use a ball when you first do any of the drills I give you. Just watch yourself and get used to the motion. When the swing becomes easy to make, then add a ball.

When you add the ball, tee it up about one-half inch above the grass, or if on a mat, use the rubber tee provided. While you are learning your swing, you should absolutely, every time, tee the ball up to make contact as easy as possible. **You *must* understand that, at this time, you will focus on sending your energy, via the club head, to the target, and not focus on contact.** Contact is so easy that you can actually hit the ball with your eyes closed (my students do this just to prove the point to themselves). You must learn to swing to the target, not at the ball, otherwise you will ruin your swing. Let the ball get in the way of a swing toward the target. This is one of the major reasons why golfers don't improve: they work on their swing, try to get the ball to a target and do everything in their power to make contact all at the same time. That's a sure formula for Attention Deficit Disorder, folks. You can't do it that way. Do not sacrifice your swing, or your awareness of the target, just to make contact. If you concentrate on the ball, the target disappears. If you concentrate on your mechanics, the target disappears. Golf is a target game. Imagine shooting darts without knowing where the dart board is. That's how most golfers play golf. No wonder the average golf score is 107!

When you are ready, introduce the ball. When things are going well with the ball teed up, put the ball on the ground and try hitting to a small target. Use your pitching address now. Use other balls out on the range as targets, and hit everything from short chips to thirty yard pitches and try to land the ball you are hitting on top of your target ball. For the most effective practice, go through your pre-shot routine (**See it, Feel it, Do it**), and switch targets each ball. You need to learn how far the ball will go using the Half Backswing, so that you have a benchmark distance you can count on, and to which you can add length as required for longer pitches. For instance, if you know that your Half and Half Swing carries the ball twenty yards, and you have a thirty yard shot, you will have a good idea of how much you will have to add to the Half Backswing to hit the ball the extra ten yards.

IMPORTANT: You cannot and should not hit the ball very far with the Half and Half Swing. The maximum distance this shot should travel is 30 yards in the air. That's not very far, but that's OK, this drill is going to enable you to hit the ball quite far real soon.

Also realize that you have to allow for the ball to roll after it hits, you don't want to fly the ball all the way to the hole. I know that's a little obvious, but I felt I should say it. The best way to get a feel for how much the ball will roll is to hit lots of pitches to a real green, and pay close attention to how the ball lands and rolls. You'll probably find it difficult to find a good practice green where pitching is allowed, so the next time you go to the course, you might want to ignore your score and hit a couple of extra pitches each hole. Just be careful not to do that when other golfers are waiting behind you, or you might find golf balls raining around you.

THE THREE QUARTER BACKSWING

When it comes time to hit longer pitches, you will need to lengthen your backswing. **Three Quarter Backswing** will give you a second benchmark distance, to which you can add or subtract as needed. Perhaps your Three Quarter Backswing carries the ball fifty yards and you have thirty five yards to your target. You know that the correct length backswing is somewhere between Half, and Three Quarter, so you can make a very educated guess as to the right length backswing.

Mechanically speaking, many people ruin their golf swing before they ever get near impact. They have difficulty extending and properly setting their wrists on the backswing. This drill, done slowly and accurately, really speeds the learning of one of the most complex motions in the golf swing. Once again, not only do you learn a vital short game skill, but you work on your swing at the same time. I love this job!

OK, here we go. Let's do this from **full swing address** first, then turn it into a pitch.

Start your backswing with your Iron Triangle, just as in the Half and Half Swing. Instead of stopping when the club shaft gets to parallel, use your right hand to point the club up to the sky. That's called the **wrist set** (or wrist cock). The butt of the club should point at the target line, or between the target line and your toes. As your right hand sets the club up, your right elbow will bend in reaction. **Remember, your right elbow bends as a reaction to your wrist set.** It should not bend before you set. As your right hand points the club up, push your left hand back away from you. Feel as though you are keeping your left hand as far away from your body as you can. This pushing back will cause your shoulders to continue turning as you make your backswing. As well, it will widen the arc of your swing, giving you more power. Be sure to brace your right leg and maintain the flex you set in your right knee at address, so that **your backswing will cause your weight to shift to your right leg.**

The Three Quarter Backswing is complete when your left arm is parallel to the ground, the club shaft and left arm form a ninety degree angle, the butt of the club points either at the target line (or an extension of it), or between your toes and the target line, and your hands are in front of your right biceps muscle.

> You already know that the target line extends from the ball to the target, but it will help to imagine that the target line extends out past the target and back behind the ball.

BALL POSITION
Note the difference in ball position between the chip, Half and Half Swing, and the Three Quarter and Half Swing.

Once you complete the Three Quarter Backswing, you have only to swing the club head forward to the Half Followthrough. But before we go further, I want to make this forward swing business as clear as possible.

> **Your hands and arms start the forward swing. Your right arm extends back and down while your hands swing the club head by pushing against the club shaft. As you continue pushing back and down, the motion turns into forward, on through impact, toward the target. Your hands and arms will pull your body around behind them.**

The transition is where my instruction really differs from the norm. There almost seems to be a conspiracy against golfers, designed to keep them in need of a lifetime of lessons and new, super high tech, super high priced clubs. Everybody has different theories about how a golf club should be swung, but some of the instruction that has been offered over the years has been outrageous, and has made it all but impossible for the average student to swing the club toward the target on the forward swing. As I've said, eighty percent of all golfers slice, largely because they do what they've been told. It's as simple as this: The best way to swing the club toward the target is to extend back and down first. Any other movement will cause the club to move off-line or away from the target, requiring a compensation or adjustment in mid-swing that the average golfer simply can't make.

DRILL

The Three Quarter and Half Swing

Maintain a Wide Arc
Notice the distance between my hands and my chest. Left arm parallel to the ground. Ninety degree angle between club shaft and left arm. Hands in front of right biceps.

The First Move
Hands and arms start the club head *back* and *down* before my shoulders or hips turn forward. The club head is *behind* me. Note the directions: **Out** (right); **Down** (to the ground); **Behind** (left); **Back** is right toward you. **Forward** is toward the target.

⇩ DOWN ⇩

⇐ BEHIND

OUT ⇒

Chapter 3   Pitching 67

Impact

I am still pushing the club through impact, and my hips are responding to the pull of my arm swing by rotating in a tight pivot. The ninety degree angle between my left arm and club shaft has become a straight line.

The Followthrough

At this point, the Triangle is still intact, as I have extended my energy toward the target. It's a powerful move through the ball that you'll see in all good golfers. I have not forced my weight to shift forward, it has happened naturally.

Keys to the Three Quarter and Half Swing

Backswing

1. Your right hand sets your wrists and your left hand pushes back away from you, as you bring your hands up, even with your right biceps muscle.

2. The butt of the club points either at an extension of the target line, or between your toes and the target line (to the other side of the target line is big trouble).

3. Your left arm and club shaft form a right angle.

4. Your right knee has firmly maintained its flex, allowing your weight to shift to your right leg.

Forward swing

1. Extend your right arm back and down while you swing the club head with your hands. Just after you start the forward swing, the club head should move behind you.

2. Your body does not turn forward until you feel your hands, arms, and the club head pull it around.

3. Stop at the Half Followthrough. Check hips, Triangle, left leg, weight, and right shoulder.

Your right hand will push against the club shaft continuously throughout the forward swing to accelerate the club head through impact. Your right forearm will also thrust the club head into and through impact. Your right hand and forearm are the two major power sources in your swing. Your body's forward rotation, while necessary, is only a minor source.

Your left hand will guide and control the club face. It adds some speed to the swing, but your right hand and arm are the main accelerators.

Make Your Practice Count

Golfers often have the best intentions when they practice, but still don't improve nearly as fast as they could. Some even get worse. *How* you practice is extremely important. You are a perfect learner. You are going to learn whatever you practice, so practice perfectly. I describe two types of practice to my students: **Precision Practice** and **Haphazard Practice**.

Precision practice requires discipline. You have to make sure you practice correctly. Don't trust your feel. What you *feel* is not necessarily what you *do*. You must have some sort of objective and accurate feedback if you want to practice precisely. Videotape yourself. Get in front of a mirror. Or have a friend who knows what's right help you.

Rush through the movements without total awareness or accurate feedback, and you practice haphazardly. That's a good formula for learning bad habits. That's why so many golfers fail to improve.

Obviously, you know how I want you to practice, but you will have to keep a constant eye on yourself to make sure you *always* practice precisely. Before every swing, ask yourself, "What *am* I doing out here?" Whether you are working on mechanics, or getting the ball to a target, know what you are working on, and concentrate only on that. Don't waste your time. Chances are, you don't have much of it. You can learn the golf swing really quickly if you want to. It's all in the quality of your practice. The following is exactly how I want you to practice.

Start without a ball! You've got to be tired of hearing that by now, but are you doing it??? Make your Three Quarter Backswing and hold it. Look. Check for accuracy. Make sure it's right. When you take a look back, make sure you stay in your posture. Don't stand up straight. Then watch the club as you start the forward swing. The **club head** should move *behind* you as your hands push and your right arm extends to move the club *back* and *down*. Then allow your hips to be pulled around as you continue pushing and extending toward the target. Stop at the Half Followthrough, and check again.

It is a great help to think that you will always use the Half and Half Swing through impact. Look at it this way: On the backswing, you start with the Half Backswing; continue on up to the Three Quarter Backswing; move **back down** to the Half Backswing; and do the Half and Half Swing through impact. You take a bigger backswing only to give yourself more time to accelerate the club head (when you are ready for speed), but that does not change the way you move through impact. You will *always* swing the club head and rotate through impact as in the Half and Half Swing.

When the correct motion becomes easy and comfortable, tee balls up and hit very soft shots with little club head speed. Practice slowly and perfectly, and gradually shift your focus away from your mechanics and to the target. Don't let contact distract you. Just hit lots of balls and your contact will improve automatically. As you improve, add speed gradually, but never allow your swing to deteriorate under the pressure of speed. Your speed should reflect your competence, not your strength or athletic ability.

Once you have graduated (don't rush it!) to something close to full speed with total control and awareness of your swing, you should get more interested in where the ball goes. Now is the time to let go of your mechanics completely, and just hit the ball to a target. Concentrate on the target throughout your swing and send your energy (through the club head) toward the target. As long as your forward swing is correct (energy toward the target), the only variable left in your swing will be where the club face is aimed at impact. If the ball goes right, the club face was aimed right. If the ball goes left, the club face was aimed left. Adjust by using your hands to rotate the club face either more or less through impact to get the desired direction. More on that later. Start with a twenty yard wide target, and try to hit balls within that area. As you improve, make your target smaller.

Then you are ready to hit pitches with the ball on the ground. Use **pitching address**. Contact is simply a matter of too low, too high, or just right. Don't give contact too much thought. It's just a matter of practice. Keep adjusting. Allow your wonderful mind to learn from the feedback contact gives you. When you hit the ground before the ball, that's called a "fat" shot. The adjustment is to swing higher next try. When you hit the top of the ball and roll it, that's called a "topped" shot. The adjustment is to swing lower. Golf is not rocket science, folks. Just keep adjusting and learning. And when you hit a particularly awful shot, laugh it off. Don't take this game too seriously.

As soon as you are able, find out what distance you can consistently hit sand wedge shots with the Three Quarter Backswing. Use that distance as a benchmark and then adjust the backswing length to hit those pitch shots which are between Half Backswing and Three Quarter Backswing lengths. Pick out balls on the range to use as targets. Go through your pre-shot routine (**See it**, **Feel it**, **Do it**) and change targets each shot. You need to get so good with your pitches that you can put the ball to within ten feet of the target all day long.

Watch Out for These Mistakes

Too Much Backswing
A larger backswing than the distance requires will cause you to decelerate on the forward swing. You'll have trouble with contact and distance control. Keep it short and sweet.

Lunging at the Ball
This is really just a spine angle change. Make sure you do not allow your head to drop down during the forward swing, or you will experience what I call "ground effect;" the classic fat shot.

Iron Triangle Breakdown
This is a biggie. If you are extending toward the target on the forward swing, you should not experience this flaw. But if you experience technical difficulty, spend a lot of time on the Half Followthrough.

Congratulations!

Recognize the fact that you know what you are doing, and that, while you will still have to practice the mechanics of pitching, it's time to spend more of your practice time concentrating on the target, rather than on your swing. Remember, the object is to master the mechanics so that you can move on (graduate, if you will) to playing golf.

I certainly realize that there are a lot of mechanics to learn in golf, and I've done my best to help you learn the proper mechanics throughout this book, but you must make a clear distinction, and it's not so easy, between golf and golf mechanics. Mechanics are your ABC's, golf is writing.

4
THE FULL SWING

The feature of this book that I like most is how we build your golf game, starting with the putt and ending with the full swing. The short game and the full swing all rely upon the same fundamentals. As you have learned the essential short game techniques, you have also been building your swing. Isn't that a great deal? We are now ready to complete your swing, and that will be easy because your fundamentals are so solid by now.

Realize that you'll have to grind a bit at first, but your efforts will be rewarded with a fine golf swing.

The Importance of a Model

Having a clear swing model in your head (and sticking to it) is essential to your learning and continued improvement. There is so much information out there that golfers go to the course with several different swings in their head and can't decide which one to use. This indecision causes a lack of trust and, of course, the inability to focus purely on the target. Learn your swing once, and then use it for the rest of your life. You *will* have to fine tune it from time to time, but do not change your basic swing concept ever! This swing works, and it's simple. You just have to practice it until it becomes yours. You will need some sort of feedback (video is best) so that, when you make your swing without thinking about it, it *is* the model. By the way, another pitfall to avoid is to judge your progress while you are progressing. You can only notice improvement in retrospect, and so you must be patient with (and non-judgemental of) yourself while you learn. You are on the right path. Stick with it and enjoy the ride.

Ignore all the myriad swing theories out there, and let yourself learn this extremely efficient method to the point of ownership. Then turn your attention to the target and send your energy toward it. Don't worry about contact. You'll learn to make good contact automatically. The effort to hit the ball is what destroys most golfers in the first place. From day one, golfers concern themselves almost entirely with hitting that little ball, completely oblivious to the fact that they have to send it to a target. So they improve their ability to hit the ball, but not their ability to play golf. It doesn't have to be that way.

Here's what you need to do...

7 Steps to Good Golf

1. **Choose a good model for your game.** All learning occurs through a model. The model in this book is as simple as it gets and, most importantly, it works.

2. **See the model clearly in your head.** Study the model until you can see the complete motion in your mind's eye. Know where the club is supposed to be throughout the motion. Know where *you* are supposed to be. You must have no "blind spots" in your view of the model.

3. **Become the model.** Practice. Train your body to automatically seek the proper position. This will take some time. Sorry, I cannot tell a lie.

4. **Use your swing to send the ball somewhere.** Introduce a ball only after you can consciously control the club (put it in the right place). Separate mechanics from golf. Swing to the target and watch what happens. Think "Hmmm, that's neat, let's send it over that way a little more." Practice becomes preparation for play.

5. **Trust yourself and play.** Stop working on your swing and "just do it." Focus on the target and send your energy there. Play.

6. **Decide how good you want to get, and commit to a practice and play schedule that suits your goal.** The better you want to get, the more time you will have to spend. This might actually be step one.

7. **Make sure you spend at least one-half of whatever practice time you have on the short game.**

As far as the first five steps go, it is important, imperative actually, that you go in order. Most people go straight to Step 5, and never do get very good at the game. They end up giving up in frustration, thinking that golf is too difficult for them. Golf is not rocket science, it just has to be approached properly.

I don't mean to imply that this is going to be a cake walk for you. You are sure to have your ups and downs, but you can now take a more long-term view of your golf game, realizing that you are on the right path to good golf. And that's a whole lot better than floundering away with no clear idea of what you are trying to do in the first place. Be patient, and choose to have fun learning and playing. Play at learning. Play at practicing. Play at playing. Don't work at playing. We already work enough.

The Turn

Most of the problems golfers have stem from not turning properly. When you make a poor turn, the club never gets into good position at the top of the backswing, and poor position at the top is almost impossible to recover from. Another neat feature of this book is that my students rarely have problems with the turn after they learn the Half and Half Drill and the Three Quarter and Half Drill, but I still want to make it clear, just in case you ever run into problems.

Keys to a Good Backswing Turn:

At the top of the backswing:

Important: It is OK for your head to move as much as two inches to the right as you make your backswing. Do not try to keep your head perfectly still. Doing so may cause you to make a poor turn.

1. Spine tilts slightly to the right.
At address position, your spine tilts slightly to the right. At the top of your backswing, your spine should still tilt to the right. The correct feeling is that your spine is the center of your swing and that you turn around your spine. You want to maintain your spine angle throughout your swing.

2. Left shoulder is lower than the right.
A line across your shoulders is perpendicular to your spine, right? Imagine the letter "T." That's what your shoulder line and spine look like. When your shoulders turn, they will remain perpendicular to your spine. From address position, your shoulders "seesaw" around your spine. The left shoulder is lower on the backswing and the right shoulder is lower on the forward swing.

3. Left shoulder is behind, or at least even with, the ball.

How far you turn is a matter of flexibility. You may find that, due to a lack of flexibility, you cannot get your left shoulder to the ball without lifting your left heel off of the ground. In this instance I suggest allowing the left heel to come up a little, but no more than necessary.

4. Your weight is firmly on your right leg.

It is vitally important that you maintain the flex in your right knee as you turn to make the backswing. If you do not, your weight shift will be thrown off, and you will invite a whole bunch of problems into your swing. Your right leg is the main support of your backswing. As you turn back to the right, your weight should move to your right heel. Your right knee must maintain its flex in order to receive your weight. You want to feel like your upper body is leaning over your right leg just a little.

Important: Your legs are the foundation of your swing. Just as a your house needs a solid foundation, so does your golf swing. Your right leg is the main support of your backswing and your left leg is the main support of the forward swing.

Watch your hip movement. Your hips should rotate as though you had a barbecue skewer right on up through your body in place of your spine. Do not let your hips slide to the right or left.

One Good Turn...

Left shoulder behind the ball and lower than the right. Weight firmly on braced right leg. My upper body appears to be leaning ever so slightly to the right, because I have maintained the spine angle that I had set at address. Practice your turn regularly. If it's not right, neither is your swing.

DRILL

THE LEVEL TURN

Standing straight up, rest the club on your shoulders. If you can, rest it across your shoulderblades.

Turn back to the right as on a backswing. Keep the club on both shoulders and allow your weight to shift onto your right heel.

Check for these keys:

1. Try to get your left shoulder over your right foot.

2. As you turn back, your left knee should be pulled in toward your right knee, with your left foot preferably flat on the ground.

3. **Your weight should move to the heel of your right foot. Feel that your right leg is "loaded" with weight.**

The club should move parallel to the ground throughout this drill. Because you are standing straight, your spine is perpendicular to the ground. Your shoulder line is perpendicular to your spine, therefore your shoulder turn is **level** (parallel to the ground) in this drill. This condition will change as soon as you get into address position.

Now turn forward.

When you finish, check for four keys:

1. **Your left leg should be totally straight and holding almost all of your weight.**

2. **Your right hip should be above your left foot if possible.**

3. **Your right shoe should be up on its toe, almost weightless.**

4. **Your spine should still be straight. There should be a straight line down the front of your body from your chest to your left foot.**

I realize that doing turn drills is not all that fun, but if your turn is not correct, you are in for big problems. Start each practice session with these drills, as a warm-up. You'll probably play better than without doing them, and you'll improve the quality of your golf swing at the same time. That's a pretty good deal!

THE LEVEL TURN
Shoulders remain level (perpendicular to your spine) throughout. Try to keep your eyes straight ahead of you on the way back, but let them move forward, as though following the ball's flight, on the way forward.

DRILL

ADDRESS POSITION TURN DRILL

Now try the same drill from address position. Because you have inclined your spine to get into your address, your shoulder turn is no longer level to the ground, but on an angle which is still perpendicular to your spine. Your left shoulder, therefore, ends up lower than your right on the backswing, and your right shoulder ends up lower than your left on the forward swing. Make sure you still have that straight line down the **front** of your body at the finish, as above. That's very important.

FRONT VIEW AT ADDRESS

BACKWARD TURN: Left shoulder low; weight firmly on right leg; spine tilts slightly to the right.

FORWARD TURN: Straight line down the front of the body; right shoulder low; left leg straight, supporting almost all my weight.

SIDE VIEW AT ADDRESS

BACKWARD TURN: Maintain flex in right knee; spine angle is the same as at address.

FORWARD TURN: Hips face the target; right foot up on toe and weightless; spine angle is consistent.

The Belly Button Turn

Insert the butt of the club into your belly button so that it is perpendicular to your stomach, and take hold of the club out on the shaft so that your arms form the Iron Triangle. Using only your shoulders and hips, with zero hand and arm action, turn to the right, keeping your feet flat on the ground, until you can turn no more. The club should still be perpendicular to your stomach. Now turn forward. Again, the club should still be stuck in your belly button and perpendicular to your stomach. Remember to keep your right leg firm on the backswing. On the forward turn, stop and check your finish.

Once again:

1. **Your left leg should be totally straight and holding almost all of your weight.**

2. **Your right hip should be as close to above your left foot as possible.**

3. **Your right foot should be up on its toe, almost weightless.**

4. **There should be a straight line down the front of your body from your chest to your left foot.**

BELLY BUTTON DRILL
Keep the club shaft perpendicular to your stomach as you turn your body. Don't use your hands at all, other than to hold onto the club, of course.

The Full Backswing

As I've said, you already know the turn, most of the backswing, and how to swing the club forward, all you have to do is add the correct position at the top of your backswing and the finish to what you already know, and you are done with your mechanics!

How to ruin your learning:

Introduce the ball, and the concept of contact, before you master the technique. Yeah, well, I'm tired of saying it, too.

OK. Start at address position and go to your Three Quarter Backswing. Your full backswing is almost complete from here, all you need to do is finish your turn and lift your arms a little. Your position at the top sets you up for the forward swing. You can either make the forward swing difficult or you can make it easy, all by where you put your arms and the club at the top. The full backswing checkpoints are as follows.

1. Left shoulder points at or behind the ball.
You know that already, but let me make it clear. You must make a good turn to make a good golf swing. It's that simple.

2. Left shoulder lower than the right.
Do not *try* to get your left shoulder down, that may cause a spine angle change. Your address position should make the left shoulder low condition automatic. Maintain your spine angle.

3. Weight firmly on your right leg.
Maintain the flex in your right knee. Your right leg is your body's support structure on the backswing.

4. Left arm is across your shoulder line (perpendicular to your spine) and quite straight.
With your left arm across your shoulder line, you can start your forward swing by extending back and down as we have already discussed. If your left arm is above your shoulder line, you will have to make a loop in your forward swing to swing the club along the correct path. If your left arm is below your shoulder line, your swing will come too much from the inside, causing you to hit the ball too far out to the right. We will discuss the club path more in-depth a little later. For now, you'll just have to take my word for it. Your left arm should be as straight as you can make it without forcing it straighter than it wants to go. If it bends a little, that's OK. Just don't let it collapse on you.

5. Club shaft is just about parallel to the target line.
I could get real technical here, but I won't. I do not think it is vital to have the club shaft perfectly "on-plane" (parallel to the target line) at this stage of your game.

6. Right elbow is bent about ninety degrees.
Watch out for over-bending your right arm. You can cause your left arm to break down, as well as get your right elbow into bad position.

7. Right forearm points just about straight down to the ground.
How close you get your right forearm to straight down depends upon your flexibility. The closer you can get to straight down, the easier the forward swing will be. Just as with the straight left arm, do not force anything. Forcing leads to undue tension, which will make it difficult for you to make a good swing.

Do you *really* want to make this game as easy as possible? Then get this top of the backswing position right. Study the following pictures and try to do the same thing. Practice in front of a mirror so that every backswing you make is perfect, and soon you will think you've been doing it that way your whole life. It really does not take long to make new habits, in fact, the habituation process only takes twenty-one days. Give me between sixty and one hundred perfect practice swings a day for three weeks, and you won't have to worry about this mechanical stuff any more.

Make your practice swings count. Whatever you practice is exactly what you'll learn, so practice precisely. Go slowly and try to get into the right position without having to adjust it, and you'll be fine.

Realize that I have certain physical limitations which are different than you, so we will both look different although we try to attain the same position. Once again, do not force your body. Freedom from excess tension is more important than duplicating my position exactly. Come as close as you can to the model, staying within your body's limitations.

At the Top

At the Top, Front View
Spine tilts slightly to the right, as it did at address; left shoulder is behind the ball; right elbow is bent just about 90°, creating a gap between my hands and my head.

At the Top, Side View
Left arm across shoulders; right forearm is almost straight down; right knee remains flexed; spine angle is the same as at address, making the left shoulder lower than the right (note angle down left side).

At the Top, Behind View
This view provides a better look at the right elbow at the top. Notice that, from this view, the right elbow appears to be in front of my chest.

LISTEN. I know what you're going to do. You'll go to the range and try to make this swing while hitting balls. **WRONG!** You won't learn correctly with a ball in the way. Practice your swing in front of a mirror and make sure you are getting the mechanics right. Don't go to the range with these pictures in mind and try to hit balls *thinking* that you are doing it right. You'll be very surprised at how well and how quickly you learn if you follow these instructions, but you have to do it right!!!

The Forward Swing

The reason I have been so particular about the position at the top, is that the forward swing is made far simpler when started from a good backswing. It is bad science to attempt error correction on the way to the ball. Of course, it *is* kind of fun to watch.

The forward swing is exactly the same as in the Three Quarter and Half Swing, except in the full swing, you won't stop at the Half Followthrough. Swing the club head through impact by extending your right arm back and down as your hands push the club shaft, and keep pushing and extending toward the target, until your arms and hands pull your body around to a full and balanced finish. All other motion in the swing is subject to, and results from, the movement of your arms and hands.

The quickest way to disrupt your forward swing is to turn either your hips or your shoulders first. If you turn first, you will instantly and unavoidably move your hands **out** first, rather than **back and down**. Although it may seem instinctive to throw everything you have at the ball right from the start of the forward swing, you must realize that the properly timed sequence of motions is far more efficient than brute force. The difference between what moves first in the forward swing is subtle, and requires acute awareness to be certain of what actually happens.

Although I will try to convey the **feel** of the forward swing, do not trust your feel alone. Watch yourself closely so that you actually **do** what you **feel** you are doing. What you feel you do and what you actually do are often very different things.

The Magic Move
If ever there was one "magic" move, this is it. Get the club shaft in line with your right forearm half way down to the ball for maximum speed and control. Almost all pros get here, but few club golfers do.

Forward Swing Keys

1. Extend your right arm back and down as your hand push (swing) the club shaft.
Feel that you are getting the club head as far away from you as possible as you swing. The wider your swing arc, the more room you have to accelerate *and* the straighter the club moves through impact. A wider arc, therefore, gives you both more power and more control. Another good thought for the forward swing is to push your right hand away from your right shoulder as you swing.

2. As you extend back and down, the club shaft moves inside your right shoulder.
Turn your head and watch, or look in a mirror. See it happen. If you see the club shaft between your shoulder and neck half way down, you did not extend back and down properly.

3. Club shaft lay over the right forearm.
This is the "on-plane" look we are striving for. Once again, please check yourself, and make sure you are getting the club here. You'll thank me later.

SET FOR TAKE-OFF
Left arm across the shoulder line. Swing the club head right from here (begin releasing now).

EXTEND BACK AND DOWN
Right arm extends back and **straight** down, while hands push the. Note that as I extend, the club shaft moves inside of (left of) my right shoulder.

CLUB SHAFT OVER RIGHT FOREARM
Swing is on-plane, club head is behind me. Shoulders and hips just begin to feel the arms pull them into motion.

4. Impact. The moment of truth.
The "power angles" you set at the top of the swing (the wrist set and right elbow bend) have been released into straight lines.

5. Followthrough.
Extension toward the target. Send your energy (through the club head) toward the target.

6. Finish in balance.
Balance equals control. Hold your finish on every shot.

Here are two real good thoughts to keep in mind:

Feel as though you are swinging through water.
Keep pushing that club all the way through impact. Right now you should be going very slowly, but with the idea that you will gradually accelerate from the top of the backswing, all the way through impact.

Do not hit *at* the ball, swing the club to the target.
The effort to make contact can cause you to change your swing. You want to be only remotely aware that the ball is even there while you make your swing. The idea is to *swing toward the target and let the ball get in the way.*

FULL RELEASE AT IMPACT	FOLLOWTHROUGH	FINISH
You can't see it from here, but my arms have straightened out into impact. My forward motion has caused my hips to turn slightly toward the target.	Hips and shoulders are pulled around as right hand continues extending out to the target.	Perfect balance, the sign of total control.

How to Practice Your Forward Swing

You already know that you are supposed to practice without a ball until the perfect motion is comfortable. When it comes to the full swing, the ball can make golfers do some really weird things. Just watch some of the other golfers at the range. Before you are ready to hit a ball, go slowly and perfectly through the drills until you feel that you own them. Then, add a ball and do these drills slowly and perfectly *and send your energy to your target*. Even hit some balls with your eyes closed, keeping the target clear in your mind as you send your energy toward it. Then be certain to maintain your swing's quality as you gradually add speed, but do not rush yourself. Add pace only when you can "pure it" at the current speed more often than not. Pure it means you hit the ball accurately and on the sweet spot of the club. You'll know when you hit the sweet spot, because the club won't vibrate in your hands.

People really mess themselves up when they add the ball or speed too soon. Impatience is your greatest adversary. You must have total control of the golf club if you want to play well. You will be far better able to control the club if you are **consciously aware** of the club's position throughout the swing. So go slowly and feel exactly where that club is. When it comes time for a ball and a target to be introduced, you need to forget your mechanics and concentrate on the target. Hence, do not introduce the ball and target too soon, or you will set yourself up for frustration. The swing, the ball, and the target are just too many things to think of at the same time. You can make golf as hard as you want, but you don't have to. It's all in the manner in which you learn the game.

The full speed golf swing happens too fast to consciously control, therefore it is very difficult to work on your swing at full speed. While you practice your swing, first watch the club move and make sure you move it correctly, and *then* feel what the correct swing feels like. Get the mechanics right first, and then translate those mechanics to feel. Practice makes permanent. Only *perfect* practice makes perfect.

> If you play a musical instrument, you know what the learning process is all about. You start a new piece of music and slowly labor over it as you learn the notes, because your fingers just don't know where to go. As you become more comfortable with the music and more competent at finding the right notes, your speed naturally increases, without any effort. Similarly, in golf, your speed must reflect your competence, not your desire to "kill" the ball. That's the way to approach your golf game.

Mastering the Forward Swing

The golf ball only knows how good impact was. It doesn't know what kind of clubs you use, and it doesn't know if you are tall or short, weak or strong. It doesn't even know if you fall down after you hit it. Your forward swing creates impact, and so your success in golf is directly related to the quality of your forward swing. These drills are designed to help you master the forward swing. They should be done at every practice session until you are finished habituating your golf swing, and then should be included as part of your regular practice routine, to help you maintain your swing.

Take a Look

Your eyes are a very valuable source of feedback for teaching yourself correctly. Don't hesitate to look back from time to time to confirm the quality of your swing. If you don't check yourself, you may teach yourself the wrong thing, and that's why so many golfers have such difficulty with the game.

DRILL

THE RELEASE

At the top, you set two "power angles" which represent stored energy. They are the angle between the club shaft and left arm (wrist set), and the right elbow bend. Both angles are about ninety degrees. The club head gains speed as the angles straighten, and reaches full speed when the angles become straight lines. The "release," then, refers to straightening out the angles into impact. That's done by uncocking your wrists gradually and straightening your right arm. Many golfers consider the rotation of the club face through impact to be the release, but that is not so.

Contrary to current instruction, you want to begin The Release immediately as you start the forward swing. "Hold the angle" and the "late release" are instructions which are actually the opposite of what great players do. Witness the bending of the club shaft at the top of the backswing in nearly all great players. The bend comes from pressure against the shaft. The pressure comes from the hands releasing. The only way to bend (load) the shaft is to release.

THE RELEASE
Begin releasing (straightening the power angles) right from the start of the forward swing. Shoulder and hip rotation should occur as a response to the release. Do this drill. I implore you. DO THIS DRILL!!!

Chapter 4   The Full Swing 91

Complete your backswing and stop at the top. Gradually uncock your wrists as you extend your right arm back and down. Come to an abrupt stop at impact, where the club shaft and left arm form a straight line. The key to the Release drill, is to control the motion so completely that your hips and shoulders move only when they must, and so all movement occurs in the proper sequence.

It is important to realize that this drill exaggerates The Release to the point that you will most probably find the left arm/club shaft angle becomes fully released (a straight line) earlier than you would actually like. Don't worry, that's fine for now. You are not using much arm speed yet, and so The Release is early. But when you notch up your arm swing to full speed, The Release will be just right. In fact, the only way you *can* release too early is if you don't swing your arms quickly enough. With that said, there *is* a proper blend between uncocking the wrists and swinging the arms. You must not just uncock your wrists to start the forward swing, you must extend back and down while you uncock. The motion needs to be smooth and needs to flow. You should feel your arms just start to pull your hips into motion as your hands approach impact.

The Release is one of the most successful drills I have ever seen to teach the correct feel for the start down. Don't absentmindedly do the drill, be very aware that your hands and right arm do, indeed, start the motion.

DRILL

The Full and Half Swing

Up to this point, we have been stopping at the top of the backswing and then starting the forward swing. Now we will add the **Transition**, which is the smooth change of directions from the backswing to the forward swing. I want you to go, ever so slowly, to the top of your backswing. As soon as you reach the top, start the Forward Swing just as slowly and continue on through impact to the Half Followthrough and stop. Be very aware of the completion of the backswing and the start forward. Did you feel your right arm extend and the release? Or did you feel your shoulders turn first? Did you move your hips first? Did the club head get behind you on the way down? Did you extend your energy toward the target? Open up your feelers.

While you do this, you must be certain that you are doing it correctly. As I've already said, that's why I want you to go slowly. The mechanics must precede the feel. Now you know the mechanics and are ready to translate those good mechanics into feel. You must learn to flow from the top of the backswing, through impact, and on to the Half Followthrough.

FULL AND HALF SWING

Slow but continuous motion from address to the Half Followthrough. The Followthrough will be a little higher now, due to increased momentum gained from a longer swing. (I've gone very slowly for the pictures creating insufficient momentum to carry me to a higher Followthrough).

Chapter 4   The Full Swing   93

I want you to start forward in the slowest motion possible and then gently and gradually accelerate through impact, toward the target. Avoid trying to hit the ball far right now, and focus your attention on swinging toward the target. As you master this drill, you can add speed gradually, but always with a slow start and continuous acceleration through impact. Hold and check your Half Followthrough for accuracy.

Know what you are working on and evaluate only that. Right now, you are working on making a slow, flowing, perfect forward swing with the intention of sending your energy to the target via the club head. As I have said, contact is just a matter of practice. Don't give it a thought. Keep swinging to the target and contact will come naturally. It is inaccurate to evaluate the quality of your swing based on the feedback you get from contact. Soon enough, you will reach a level where you can and should work on ball flight, but not yet.

Let me make something clear. Do you remember when I said that some motions create other motions? Well, in the forward swing, your shoulders are not *totally* motionless, they have to move some, but that movement is ***passive***, and results directly from the ***active*** movement of your arms and hands. Your arms are connected to your body, so when one moves the other must respond. Your job is to move your arms and hands and let the rest of your body respond as it needs to. You will have to be very aware of the transition to get it right. Feel, for certain, that your arms and hands control the forward swing, and that your body's rotation forward occurs well after you start forward.

The Ball Goes Where You Hit It!

Note the forward extension in the far right picture on this page; it's going out toward the target, right where I want the ball to go. Makes sense, huh?

THE FINISH

You are now ready to complete your swing. Your fundamentals are solid, although you may still have to think about them. Maintain your diligent practice and it will be worth it. If you will practice your swing just sixty times a day for twenty-one days in a row, you will own it.

Your **finish** (what most people call the "followthrough"), is largely a product of what comes before it, and greatly depends upon the club head speed you generate during your swing. When you increase your speed, you will complete your finish.

The finish is not necessarily a position to strive for in itself, but if you do things right, you will end up very similar to the checkpoints below. Hold your finish after each shot for the rest of your golf career.

Finish Checkpoints:

1. **Perfect balance. Balance *is* control.**
2. **Left leg straight with almost all of your weight on it.**
3. **Hips face the target. If you are very flexible, your right hip may be closer to the target than your left.**
4. **Club shaft touches the back of your head or your neck.**
5. **Right foot up on the toe, with almost no weight on it.**
6. **Right shoulder is a little lower than your left.**

Well what do you know, we are done with the full swing. Practice it until it becomes a habit. Remember that only perfect practice makes perfect.

Chapter 4　　　　　　　　　　　　　　　　The Full Swing 95

STORE ENERGY　　　RELEASE ENERGY　　　FINISH IN BALANCE

STORE AND RELEASE ENERGY

Conserve energy on the backswing, and expend it on the forward swing. It's very common to expend energy on the backswing through muscular tension and too much speed. You don't want to do that. The backswing is smooth and unhurried and the forward swing is a smooth and gradual acceleration to full speed (full release of energy). Don't rush.

DRILL

LATE SPEED

This is my number one drill to train and maintain your swing. The purpose is to create total awareness and control of the entire golf swing. I am absolutely amazed by how well and how quickly this drill works.

Make a backswing in slow motion, and stop at the top. Start the forward swing in slow motion, and gradually accelerate "late" into the swing. When you are ready, change directions without stopping at the top (add a smooth **Transition**). The key is to start the forward swing in *very* slow motion so that you are totally aware of your extension back and down, and that you are definitely not turning either your hips or shoulders first.

CHAPTER 4 THE FULL SWING 97

Feel the straightening of your right arm as your hands move down. Keep extending back and down in slow motion, until your hands are about belt high as in the second photos, top and bottom. Once there, gradually accelerate through the ball, toward the target, to a full finish. Look at my right arm extension toward the target in the third frame, top row. That's forward!

Say the moves out loud as you do them. "Backswing." "Hands back and down, club head behind." "Extend out to the target." "Finish." Keep the club moving at the same speed as your voice.

Start out hitting fifty yard 7 Irons until you can "pure it" more often than not, and then move up to seventy-five yards until you own it. Keep increasing the distance by twenty-five yards until you reach full speed. A full speed swing will still be a late speed swing, only the overall speed will be greater. A slow, smooth transition is necessary for all golf shots.

Full Swing Sequences

The following full swing sequences put together all that you have learned thus far. Try to imagine the flow of movement from frame to frame.

Facing View

CHAPTER 4　　　　　　　　　　　　THE FULL SWING 99

I have not included captions or explanations of the photos because I just want you to get the pictures in your head. I'd rather not clutter up these images with words.

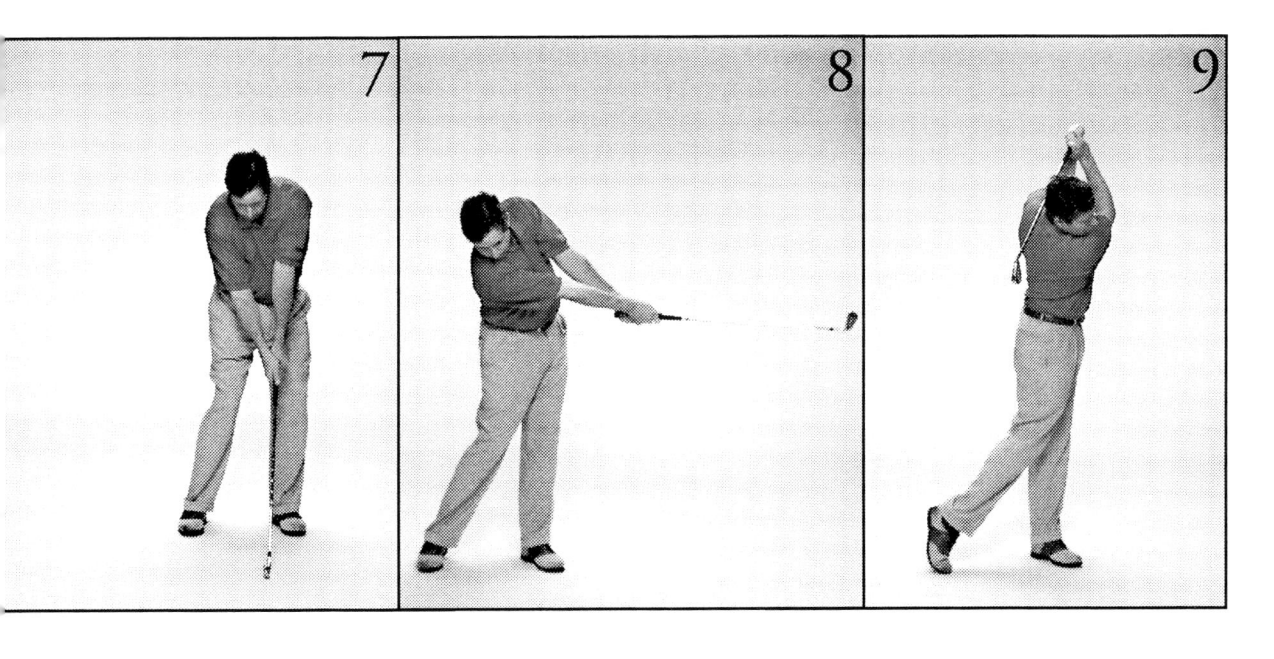

ESSENTIAL GOLF

FULL SWING SEQUENCE

TARGET LINE VIEW

Chapter 4   The Full Swing 101

Full Swing Sequence

Forward View

CHAPTER 4 THE FULL SWING 103

104 Essential Golf

Full Swing Sequence

Rear View

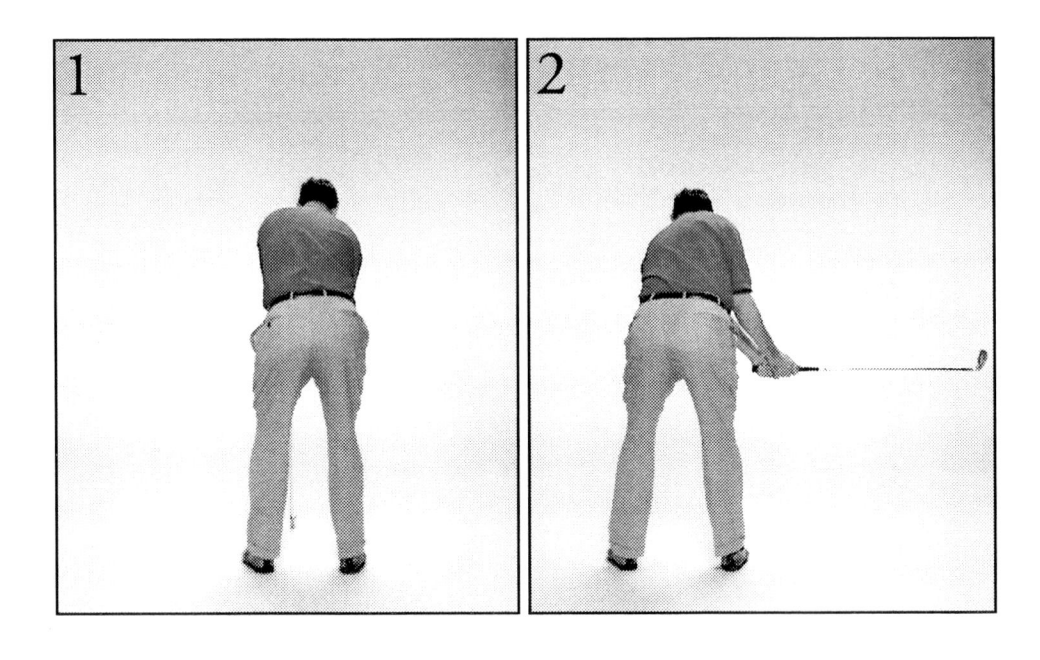

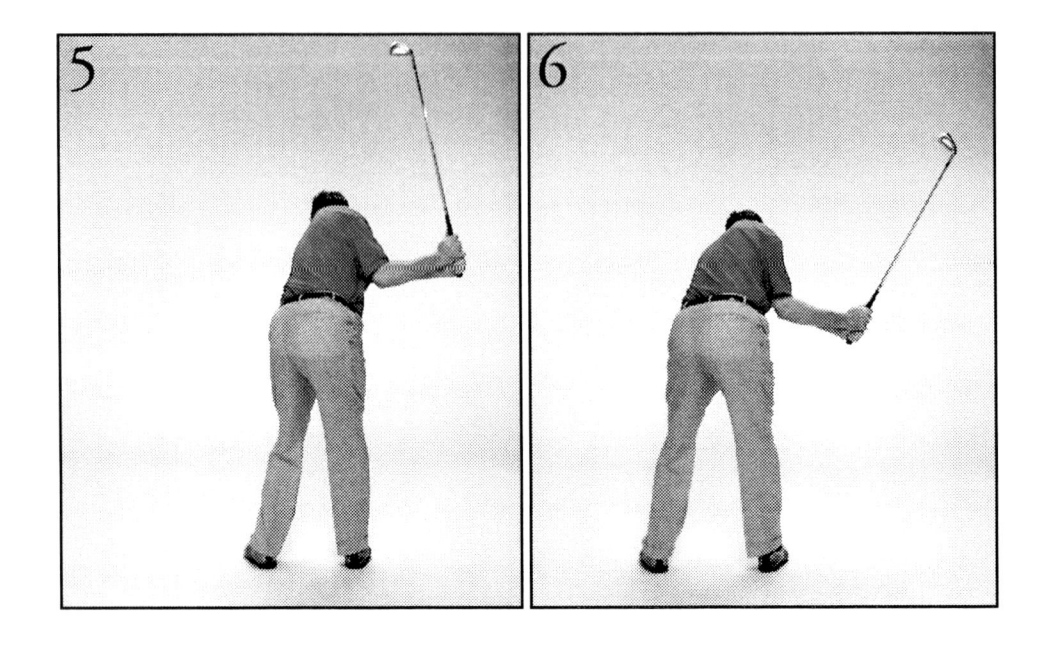

CHAPTER 4　　　　　　　　　　THE FULL SWING 105

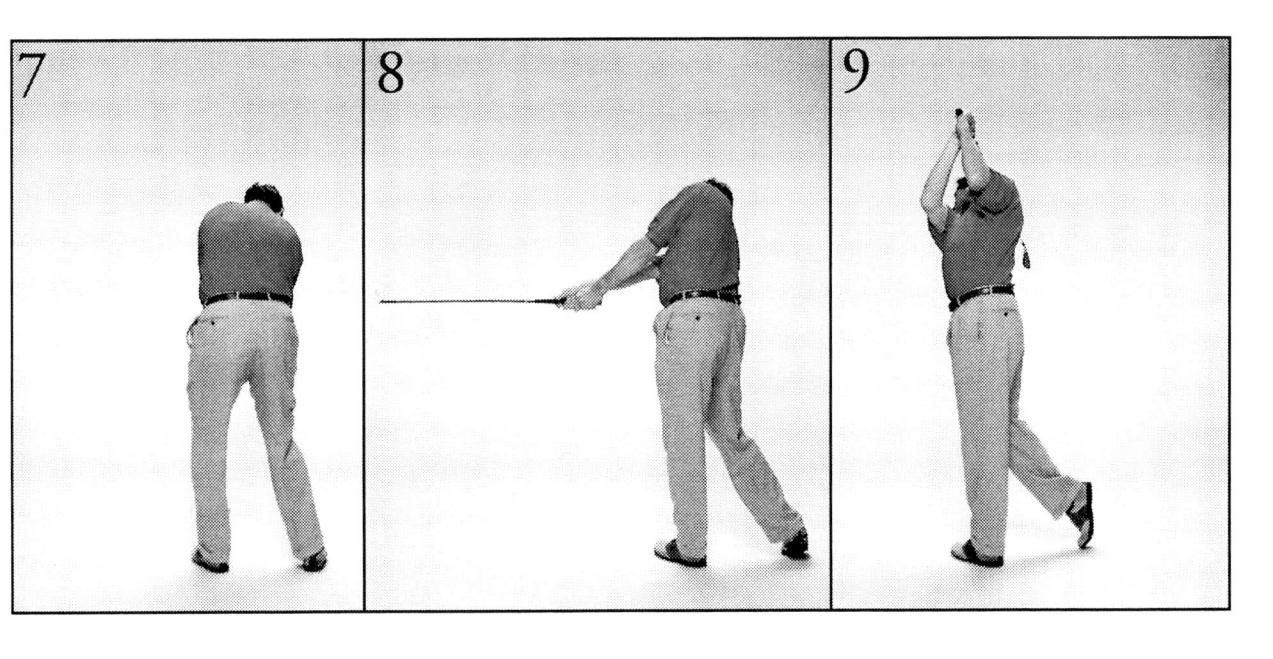

106 Essential Golf

THE FOUR KEYS TO THE

These are the four things you *must* get right in your swing. Please study these and practice them until you own them. When you video tape, or look in a mirror, you should use the Target Line view most of all; it shows you what you really need to see.

LEFT ARM ACROSS THE SHOULDER LINE

AT THE TOP

Left arm is across (parallel to) shoulder line. Left shoulder is just about over top of right foot.

ESSENTIAL GOLF SWING

Remember the Late Speed drill? Do that drill with these four keys in mind while you swing. Say them to yourself (or out loud, if you dare) as you do them. Left arm across the shoulders; push back and down; extend forward to the target; finish. Swing only as fast as you can be consciously aware of, and totally in control of, the motion.

PUSH THE CLUB BACK AND DOWN

PUSHING THE CLUB

Club shaft covering right forearm about half way to the ball (target line view). If you get the club started correctly, you almost can't go wrong.

The Four Keys to the

Extend to the Target

The Followthrough
Keep pushing the club forward, toward the target. The ball goes where you hit it, right?

CHAPTER 4 THE FULL SWING 109

ESSENTIAL GOLF SWING

FINISH IN BALANCE

THE FINISH
Body facing the target, weight on left foot, club shaft through the ears. Perfect balance is a sign of total control. Always hold your finish.

The Swing Plane

WARNING: This is advanced stuff and may be a little too technical for the new golfer. I have included it for golfers who have been at the game for some time, and need a "proof," if you will, of why I teach what I do.

You may have heard of the swing plane before, but you may not understand what it is. That's because it's usually only referred to, yet seldom, if ever, described.

I debated hard about whether to include the swing plane in this book, because it may be "information overload" for the casual golfer. It *is* a little technical. However, it may help you understand the need for the back and down start that the Forward Swing requires, as opposed to all the other theories you will hear. Most importantly, it will help you visualize exactly where the club should be throughout your swing. You will have a precise model in mind to work toward.

If this discussion confuses you, ignore it and just study the pictures. You need a clear image in your mind, but you don't need to understand why or even how this works. You need a model, that's all. The drills you have done thus far, and those to come, are designed to get you swinging the club on-plane, whether or not you know you are doing so.

The simplest way I can describe the swing plane is to say that the plane is the target line, applied to the club shaft. The on-plane club shaft is moving toward the target. So when swinging the club, we want to spend as much time on-plane as possible. When the club shaft is parallel to the ground, it is on-plane if it is also parallel to the target line. And when the club is not parallel to the target line, it is on-plane if the shaft points at an extension of the target line. My plane board (pages 112 and 113) will help clarify these two points.

The club shaft at address forms the **plane angle**. The plane board guides the club along that angle. The plane angle is on the line to the target. So, keeping the club on-plane is the same as swinging along the target line. The plane board shows us where the plane is, whether or not the club is on it.

The difficulty with swinging the club on-plane is that as you make the backswing, the club can start on-plane, but your body can keep the club on-plane only until you get a little more than half way back. To stay perfectly on-plane throughout your backswing, you'd have to stop short of three quarters back. You'd be very accurate, but you'd lack power. Instead, we

CHAPTER 4   THE FULL SWING   111

continue the backswing, which forces the club up and above the plane, creating a longer swing that allows more room to accelerate the club head.

From this "above plane" top of the backswing position, we need to return the club to the plane, thus the back and down first move I have been professing. Any other first move (and there are so many suggested moves that it's silly), will result in the club getting back on-plane late, or remaining above plane or "over the top" throughout the swing. Have you heard of "over the top" before? Now you know what it means. And that means that the club does not swing along the target line. Instead, it cuts across the target line (plane) to the left on its way through impact. That's not so good.

The benefits of getting the Forward Swing on-plane are great. The more time you have the club on-plane, the more it moves along the target line, so your accuracy improves. The on-plane club will move more level through impact, transmitting more energy toward the target rather than toward the ground (as in the over the top, slicer's swing). Swing speed is also increased as the right forearm (major source of power) and club shaft, align about half way down, and act on the ball from the same direction, and the club travels at ninety degrees to its axis of rotation (the spine). Lastly, the on-plane swing requires much less club face manipulation to get the ball to the target. It is easier to control the club face and, therefore, more consistent.

Any swing will work *if* you compensate for your errors, but if you have a regular job, I suggest you use the simplest, most effective way to swing a golf club. I'm not saying that all golfers should look exactly the same. Different body types will result in different looking swings, but all golfers should share the essentials of an efficient swing to get the most out of their talent. Otherwise, mid-swing compensations will have to be made, and that can only make golf more difficult.

Perhaps the greatest benefit of all is that once the on-plane swing becomes your model, you never again need to search for the latest hot tip, gimmick, quick fix or magic move. You simply continue to move closer to the model. Every bit closer you get, you hit the ball better *and* you understand why. That's fun. That makes golf as easy as it can get.

> **Although it may seem as though you are swinging in the wrong direction with the back and down first move, what you are actually doing is widening your arc (more club head speed), and getting the club started on the proper path to the target, (returning to your plane). But don't even think about starting the forward swing with any speed right now. Stay slow and precise. You'll learn exactly what you teach yourself.**

The Plane Truth

The plane board shows the simplest, most efficient way to swing the club. Because the club is traveling along the target line as much as possible, contact is assured, and control and power are maximized. All I must do is make the transition from the top of the backswing back to the plane and I'm set.

Yes, great golf comes out of lesser swings, but those swings are more difficult to execute and to maintain. The beauty of the this model is that the closer you get to the model, the better you hit the ball. Period. When you "lose it," you have only to check your swing on video and compare it to this, and you instantly know what to do.

Try as I might, as I complete my backswing, I cannot remain on the board, and I'm forced above it, or what's called "over the top" (photos #3 and #4). Looking at photos #4 - #6, you can clearly see that to get my forward swing back on-plane, my hands *must* first move back and down. If I turn either my shoulders or hips first, my hands will move out to the right, farther from the board. That's the slicer's swing that 80% of all golfers suffer with (shown on page 114).

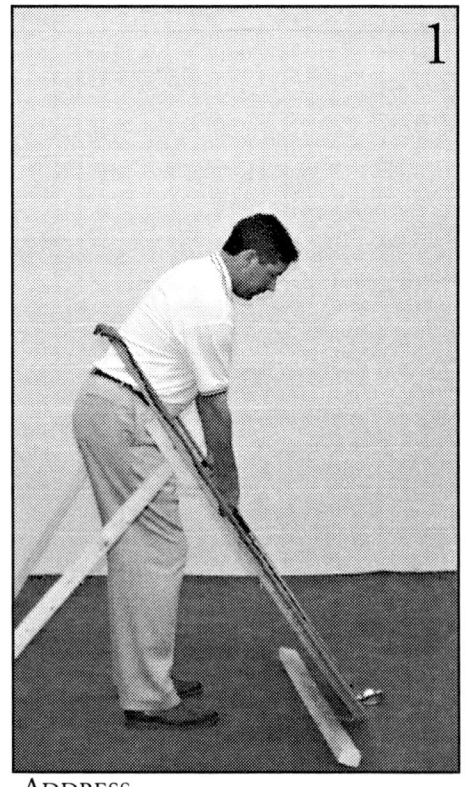

ADDRESS
Starting out right on target.

AT THE TOP
Left arm across the shoulder line. I'm well above plane and need to get back down on it.

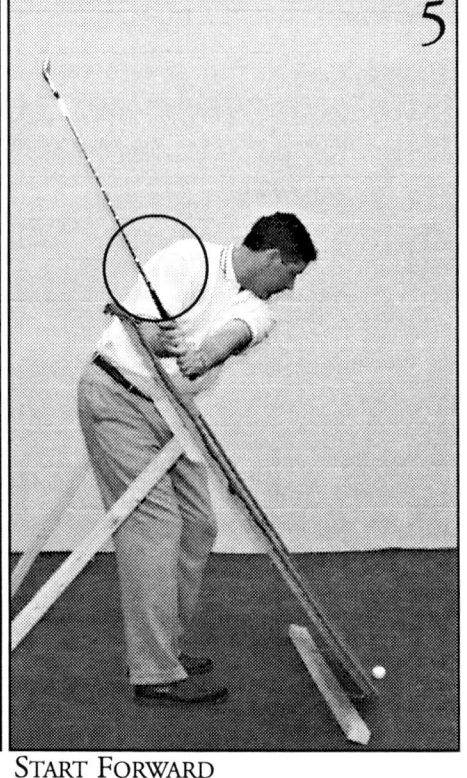

START FORWARD
Club shaft inside of (left of) right shoulder as I push the club back on plane.

CHAPTER 4 THE FULL SWING 113

2 — HALF WAY BACK
Still on-plane. Club is parallel to the ground and parallel to the target line.

3 — THREE QUARTERS BACK
I'm trying to stay on plane, but my body will not let me. I'm forced above plane.

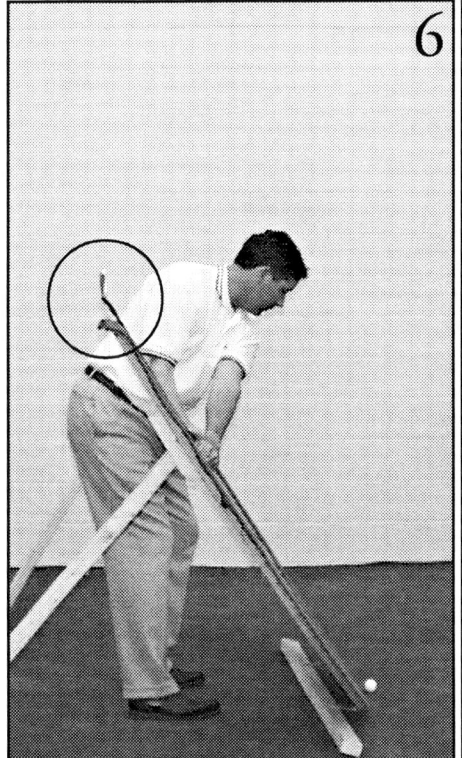

6 — HALF WAY TO IMPACT
Note club head behind my back, club shaft in line with right forearm.

7 — IMPACT
Looks a lot like address, except that my swing has forced my hips to open just a little.

Watch Out for These Mistakes

Over the Top

The classic slicer's move. Rather than start the forward swing by extending back and down, I have turned my shoulders, toward the target, causing my hands and club to move out first, and then down. The club ends up cutting across the target line to the left, resulting in either a pull, or a slice, depending upon the club face angle. Notice how "steep" (vertical) the club shaft is in photo #1. Compare these to photos #5, #6, and #7 on the previous two pages. The difference is tremendous! This is the #1 error in golf.

The Reverse Pivot

Caused by a poor turn, or losing the flex in your right leg, your weight does not shift properly to the right leg on the backswing. Rather, the weight actually moves to the left foot at the top (note how I am leaning over my left leg). Sometimes caused by attempting to keep the head rigidly still during the swing.

Too Much Backswing

Often caused by over-bending the right arm at the top. My left arm has bent considerably. My hands have gotten behind my head, narrowing my arc. I'll lose power and have more difficulty making solid contact from here.

Severely Bent Left Wrist

Your left wrist should be relatively flat at the top of your backswing. Getting the left wrist into this over-bent position, places the club face in an abnormally open position, making it difficult to square at impact. Sometimes caused by excessive rotation of the arms at the start of the backswing.

Club Shaft "Laid Off" at Top

"Laid off" is golf lingo for the club shaft pointing well left of the target line at the top of the backswing. Usually caused by over rotating the arms on the backswing or a handsy take-away, this position makes the forward swing extremely difficult. It is better to err to the other side of the target line, called "crossed-over."

IMPERATIVE!

When working on mechanics, strive to swing the club on-plane. When playing golf, forget your swing, aim at the target and swing in that direction. These may seem to be the same thing, but they are very different.

Mechanics are self-centered. Golf is target centered. Don't confuse the two.

I have a number of students who are so dedicated to improving that they forget to play golf. They think about their mechanics constantly and forget all about the target. Fixing a golf swing can take months, I realize that. But it is far more important that you learn to PLAY GOLF. If I had only one thing to say to my students, it would be this. Send your energy (via the club head) to the target. That's pretty much the idea behind everything in this book.

Congratulations!

When you are ready, and you'll know when you're ready, pat yourself on the back for a job well done and realize that it's time to let go of your mechanical thoughts and just play. Remember, that's the goal of this instruction. Learn it right, and then forget it. Now, I don't want you to think that you are finished working on your swing. But as soon as you are ready, you want to divide your practice time between working on your swing and hitting the ball to the target. They are not the same, you know.

5
FULL SWING DRILLS

As you can probably guess, I firmly believe that the fastest way to improve your golf is to combine knowledge of what to do and why to do it, with drills that teach you *how*. These are more of my favorite drills that I use to help students learn really fast. This short section is included to supplement what you have already learned. They pinpoint specific problems and can help make your practice more productive. I urge you to do all drills with the ball teed up.

LISTEN. Don't try to learn the lessons these drills teach immediately, and don't knock yourself out doing them. Just run through them during your practice sessions and allow them to gradually educate your body to do the right things automatically. The drills take time to incorporate their lessons into your swing. Don't rush. Be patient.

Golf has a way of letting us know exactly where we stand relative to where we would like to be. If you do the drills, but have difficulty maintaining your balance or making solid contact, that's no surprise. It just means you are not "there" yet. As you improve your mechanics, your contact will improve also.

DRILL

The Level Swing

If you have really tried, but are having difficulty with your golf swing, The **Level Swing** may really help you out. This drill is designed to help you teach yourself the proper movements of the swing from a position which makes the swing a little clearer to see than your normal address position. It's sort of a baseball swing, with a couple of particulars. Do this drill correctly, and you may find that your problems are solved by combining this drill and its companion, the Foot High Swing, which turns the Level swing into a golf swing.

Hold the club chest high with your arms rather straight. The club's **leading edge** should point straight up and down. Swing the club back and rotate your arms until the **club face** faces the sky.

Check for these backswing keys:

1. **Shoulders level (parallel) to the ground.**

2. **Left arm straight across the shoulder line and level.**

3. **Club shaft level.**

4. Club face leading edge level.

5. **Your right elbow should point down to the ground and should not touch your side.**

After you have the backswing correct, swing **up** to the imaginary ball that is chest high. The forward swing is very similar to a home run hitter swinging for the fences, or a topspin forehand in tennis. It's low to high.

Your arms need to rotate the **leading edge** back to its original, pointing up to the sky, position when it gets straight out in front of you (impact), and then continue to rotate until the club face faces the ground at the finish.

The **Level Swing** is exactly the same as a golf swing but by standing up straight, you will be able to more clearly see where you want to be in your swing. By doing this drill until you can flow continuously from backswing through finish, you can create excellent habits, and all you will have to do is bend down into address position and let those habits take over.

Important!!!
In order to swing up to the imaginary ball, you will first need to lower your arms toward the ground just a little to give yourself room to swing up. That is just like starting the forward swing by extending your right arm back and down.

Swinging Up
It is very similar to the baseball swing, as I've said, but a topspin forehand in tennis and throwing a hook in bowling are also helpful images.

DRILL

THE FOOT HIGH SWING

  This drill makes the transition from the Level Swing to the golf swing easy. Set up for the Level Swing, then bend from the hip joints and lower your arms until the club head is one foot above the ground. You will be in close to full swing address position, only standing a little straighter, with the club one foot above the ground.

  Make your backswing just as in the Level Swing. The only difference is that at the top of the backswing, because you have bent over into address position, your left shoulder will be lower than your right, and your left arm, the club shaft and club face will be level with only your shoulders, and *not* the ground. It is very important to realize that, due to your bent over address position, the club shaft will no longer be level with the ground at the top of the backswing, rather it will point up toward the sky.

When you start the forward swing, what used to be a low to high swing will become back and down, or what's called **inside-out**, (more on inside-out later). It is still a good idea to think of hitting up on the ball as in the Level Swing, as that thought encourages the correct path to the ball.

It may help to think of the **Foot High Swing** as an *angled* **Level Swing**. The **Level Swing** is horizontal, while the **Foot High Swing** is angled. Make absolutely certain that you do not confuse the two drills. You can ruin your swing real fast. You must remember that the club will point up toward the sky on the backswing in this drill.

The Foot High Swing also makes for a good pre-shot practice swing on the golf course. You will see some of the best players in the world make this sort of swing before or after a shot to remind themselves of the correct feel for their swing.

Approach the Ball on an Arc, not on a Straight Line
Think of making your forward swing very round through impact. That will help you get the idea of the correct shape of the swing.

DRILL

THE SWINGING START

This drill will help you flow rhythmically through your swing. After you have gotten comfortable with (and good at) your swing, you will need to switch off your mechanical mind and allow yourself to use what you know. Try this to help smooth out the bumps.

1. Start at normal address position but hover your club above the ball by an inch or so.

2. Swing the club **forward** about three feet, and then smoothly start the backswing, and continue on just as a normal golf swing. The momentum of this **swinging start** will greatly reduce the friction in your swing.

DRILL

FEET TOGETHER

Your hips should rotate above very stable legs during a golf swing, not slide back and forth. The lateral slide away from and/or toward the target (called a "sway") is a very common error that really hurts your ability to hit the ball solidly. This drill will all but eliminate swaying, teach your legs to remain sturdy through the swing, and get your hands swinging the club head.

You will be amazed by how well you can hit the ball like this, once you gain your balance.

Practice this drill every time you hit the range. It's good for you.

DRILL

Right Foot Out

This drill will help you zero out hip action so that you can work on the correct forward swing. Practice this drill if you feel your hips moving first at the start of the forward swing.

Set up with the ball centered in your stance and pull your right foot back behind your left as pictured. You'll have to gain your balance at address, but don't worry about going off balance on your finish.

This address position will "lock out" much of your lower body movement so that you can get your hands in control of the swing. Swing forward as far out to the right of the target as you can through impact.

No Way to Sway
Swaying turns the ball into a moving object and makes contact more difficult. This drill not only eliminates the sway, it also inhibits early hip movement, and gets your hands and arms moving first on the forward swing.

DRILL

Left Foot Out

This drill is designed to teach you how to properly support your weight on your right leg on the backswing. Similar to the previous drill, the Left Foot Out drill also makes it nearly impossible to start your forward swing by sliding forward, toward the target.

Use a centered ball position, but this time move your left foot back behind you and balance mainly on your right leg.

As you make your backswing, make very certain that your right leg remains rock solid, with your right knee in the same position that you had set at address. You may even want to try to "sit" or "squat" on your right knee just a little as you go back.

Swing forward as usual. Your weight will want to shift to your left foot on the forward swing. Let it.

Solid Base
Many golfers have real difficulty properly training their right leg to support their body on the backswing. This drill does it for you. Just like the previous drill, this drill also helps prevent swaying.

DRILL

RIGHT HAND ONLY

Here is a great drill to get the idea of swinging the club with your right hand and arm. Grip the club with your right hand only and make a golf swing. Make sure you allow your right elbow to bend to a ninety degree angle at the top. On the forward swing, feel your right arm extend back and down while your right hand pushes against the club shaft. Do this drill often to create a clear image of what you will do on the forward swing.

THE NUMBER ONE SOURCE OF POWER
I hit my 7 Iron 160 yards with both hands, and 130 yards with just my right hand. Hmmm. Makes you think, doesn't it?

6
PRACTICING GOLF

You are the teacher, and you *will* learn whatever it is that you teach yourself, so do your job well. Precise practice is far more important than the quantity of balls you hit. However, GOLF is different from practice, and you have to be able to move from golf swing mode, into GOLF mode if you want to play well. This chapter is here to help you make that transition.

Before I even begin, let me say that if you are still working on your grip, you are not ready to hit golf balls yet. If you still have problems with your backswing or forward swing, you are not ready for golf balls either. Please get the mechanics out of the way (mastered and then all but forgotten) before you put a ball in the way.

What Are All These Clubs for, Anyway?

The sand wedge is your short distance club. In addition to pitching, you will use this club with a full swing. Hit full shots with your sand wedge, and find out how far they fly. Then do so with every club in the bag. You need to find out your *average carry distance* (how far the ball flies in the air, excluding roll) with each club, so that you know which club to hit when you are, say, 150 yards from the hole. Learning your distances will take time, and before you can even consider distance control, you have to become proficient enough with your swing to make solid contact most of the time.

From the pitching wedge on up through the long irons, the length difference between clubs becomes a fairly predictable ten to fifteen yards. Remember, you do not need to try to hit the ball farther when using longer irons. The long irons can be more difficult to hit because they require quite a lot of club head speed to get the ball up high. If you find the 5, 4 and 3 Irons difficult to hit, you may want to try a utility club, like a 7 or 9 Wood, because the low center of gravity makes it easier to get the ball up. The larger head on these woods gives players more confidence as well.

Since you will hit more short irons than long irons during the course of a round, you should spend more practice time with the short irons.

You may find more success driving the ball with your 3 Wood rather than your Driver (1 Wood). The driver is the least forgiving club in your bag and is too difficult to control for most people. As such, I often tell students to leave the driver in the trunk. Most players will find that the added height they get with the 3 Wood actually results in more distance than they get with the driver, *and* the ball goes straighter. If you plan to use a driver, I strongly suggest that you get one with at least 10 and preferably 11 or 12 degrees of loft until you become quite a long hitter and the ball goes too high. I use a 9.5 degree.

Here's my set of clubs and the distances I carry each club.

Driver	250
4 Wood	230
2 Iron	210
3 Iron	200
4 Iron	190
5 Iron	180
6 Iron	170
7 Iron	160
8 Iron	150
9 Iron	140
Pitching Wedge	115 to 130
Gap Wedge	75 to 115
Lob Wedge	75 max, 70 most comfortable, all pitches.

This is the way *my* set works for *me*. These are *average* distances. Not the longest I have ever hit with each club, rather the distance I can safely count on every time I swing that club. You will get different distances with your set. The important thing is to find *your* distances, and don't try to equal your favorite touring pro's distances. You never want to press for distance with any club. Swing within yourself. Trying to smash a club longer than you are capable of results in some really neat looking shots, usually less distance, and, almost always, higher scores.

Between these clubs I can choke down on the club or shorten my swing to take a little distance off if necessary. Notice the gap between the 8 and 9 Iron. If I have a 145 yard shot, I will choke down an inch on my eight iron and use a full swing, to take five yards off my usual 8 Iron distance.

Approaching the Ball and the Waggle

When you are preparing to hit a shot, you will have to move into address position. The approach to the ball is often overlooked, but it is still a very important link in the chain of events leading up to the swing.

The way you move to the ball can make it easier to align yourself to the target correctly. Aim your club face before you take your stance. Stand to the side of the ball and face the target to aim your club face. Facing the target in this manner helps your accuracy in aiming the club face *and* aligning yourself. I like to complete my grip first, before I set the club down to aim it. Then I get my eyes as parallel to the horizon as possible as I aim to and lock the target.

Take your stance while loosely moving the club back and forth over top of the ball in a miniature golf swing. This movement of the club is called the Waggle, and serves two purposes: It helps get rid of shot-destroying tension, and it serves as a preview of the shot you will hit. Many amateurs freeze over the ball and get tighter and tighter until they can hardly swing the club back at all. Waggle the club until your brain tells you it's time to swing.

Here's how to approach the shot and hit it when there is a target:

Stand behind the ball and pick your target. Walk to the ball. Aim your club face first, then align yourself. Slowly look at the target while still waggling and settling into your stance. Then move your eyes slowly back to the ball. When your eyes come back to the ball, swing with only the target in mind.

Aim, Ready, Fire
I aim my club face first, and then align my body. Now I'm ready to fire. Make sure that you keep moving while you ready yourself, it will help you stay loose.

Ball Position

Ball position has to do with where the ball is placed relative to your feet. We are going to make this as simple as possible. For all full shots, the ball should be placed within two inches of your left heel. To encourage the proper angle of attack into the ball, you will simply move your right foot either closer to, or farther from, your left. The ball remains in the same position, relative to your left foot.

The short clubs require a somewhat more descending blow, that is to say, a steeper angle of attack. No, you do not have to change your swing at all. Just move your right foot so that your heels are about six inches apart. This ball position will place the ball at the low point of your swing, so that you will automatically hit slightly downward on the ball. As you move up from the wedges through the set, gradually widen your stance as you take longer clubs until you get to the driver. Your driver stance should have your feet shoulder width apart to encourage an upward approach to the ball.

One more comment about ball position: You must experiment a little to find out which works best for you. If you find your ball starting out too far to the right, move the ball a little closer to your left heel, and do just the opposite if it starts out to the left. Of course, be sure that you are making a good swing before you change ball position.

| WEDGE | SIX IRON | DRIVER |

Posture

Your posture is very important in making your swing repeatable. Many golfers make the mistake of changing their posture as they change clubs. That is unwise. Your posture sets up all the angles of your swing. If you change your posture, you change your swing. You need to use the same posture for all clubs, and just stand farther from the ball as the clubs lengthen.

WEDGE   6 IRON   DRIVER

CHAPTER 6   PRACTICING GOLF   133

CONTACT

Let me first say that the ball is what messes people up in the first place. You try so hard to hit the ball that you forget about where the target is and swing only to hit the ball. You have to swing to the target!!! I don't really want to include this in here because I don't want you to become obsessed with contact, but I've included a little section about contact just in case you are experiencing difficulty. I believe that concentration on contact is an unnecessary distraction, and you are better off just to send your energy to the target. Contact will come automatically, with experience. With that said, be patient with yourself and read on...

As you practice, you will gain experience in how to bring the club to the ball. You will need to relax and be totally non-judgemental while your brain soaks up the feedback that contact (or lack of contact) gives you. You *need* make lots of mistakes right now, so don't get too excited about what you perceive as "bad" contact.

Take a lot of practice swings and try to brush the ground without digging deep divots. Put a tee in the ground and try to hit it. When you can hit the tee repeatedly, put a ball on it. As you improve, lower the height of the tee progressively until you no longer need it. Hitting the ball consistently from the grass may take several days, weeks or months. Please don't rush the process. If you become frustrated when trying to hit the ball off the ground, put it back on a tee and get back your confidence.

Basically, contact is a no brainer: If you swing over top of the ball and miss completely, you've swung too high. Any time you hit a ball that rolls, you have swung just a little too high and contacted the ball above its equator. In both cases, swing lower. Try to hit the ground a little on the next try. If you hit the ground behind the ball, that's too low. Swing higher. I told you, this isn't rocket science.

If you are hitting the ball extremely to the right with an iron, you may be shanking the ball. Take a look at the neck (hosel) of the club and see if you have ball marks on it. If you do, simply stand a little farther away from the ball. More on shanking in Troubleshooting. If you are hitting it off the toe, move a little closer.

LISTEN. You *must* adjust. Do not allow yourself to make the same mistake repeatedly. I encourage my students to overdo the adjustment so that their brain can learn from the feedback. Contact too high should be followed by contact too low, if anything. Chances are, if you're not adjusting, you're not learning.

At this time, you may want to play golf. Feel free to tee the ball up on all shots, except those near the green, until you have confidence in your ability to make solid contact from the ground. By the way, you can't tee the ball up in a tournament, unless you are hitting a "tee shot," but it's a great idea for now.

I highly recommend that you start with a short, par three course, then graduate to a longer, executive course. Then, when you are ready, go for the full size, championship course. Remember, the object is to have as much fun as possible. Don't go get yourself beaten up by a course that's beyond your capabilities. That's no fun at all.

The Right Clubs for *You*

By this time, you are ready to get clubs that fit you, if you haven't already. Basically speaking, you need to have the correct shaft length and flex, the correct grip size, and the correct lie angle. Many golf course pro shops now offer club fitting service, using one or more of the excellent portable club fitting stations offered by leading club manufacturers. These units have several different clubs with varying lengths, flexes and lie angles for you to try, until you find the one you hit the best. Incidentally, you do not necessarily need *new* clubs. If you like your present set, they can easily be adjusted to fit you. And that's a lot less expensive than a new set.

When club fitting someone, I first look closely at their address position, not just their height, to determine the proper length shaft. Then I check swing speed and look to see how much the student loads (bends) the shaft at the top of the swing. That helps me determine the right shaft flex. I check grip size by looking to see whether the left hand fingers rest against the palm rather than digging in or not touching at all. Finally, I have them hit a few balls from what's called a lie board, which best indicates the proper lie.

Since most clubs come in only regular or stiff flexes, most of my students get the correct shaft. Tall players over six feet *may* need longer than standard clubs. Short players under five feet, six inches *may* need shorter than standard. Petite clubs are also offered by many club manufacturers for players under five feet.

The most important club fitting variable is probably the lie angle, and that should be done with a lie board which shows you where the sole of the club contacts the ground. I put duct tape on the sole of the club and have the student hit balls off of the lie board, which is just a flat board placed on the ground like a hitting mat. After the two balls are hit, I look at the sole of the club to see where the mark left by contact with the board, not the ball, is. If the mark is in the center of the sole, it fits. A mark out on the toe means the club is too flat, and will cause an otherwise good shot to go to the right. Conversely, a mark on the heel means the club is too upright, and will cause the ball to go to the left. Most clubs can have the lie angle adjusted to properly fit you, but you must get to a lie board to find out what lie you need. Do not trust a finger tip to floor measurement. The lie angle you require depends more upon your swing than your height and arm length.

The significance of lie angle cannot be overstated. For every degree too upright or flat, the ball will go eleven feet left or right of the target on a 150 yard shot. To play well with clubs that do not fit you requires that you compensate in some way for the ill fitting equipment. Golf's hard enough. Get your clubs fit to you. A good club fitter or a competent PGA golf professional will be able to help you find the right clubs.

CHAPTER 6   PRACTICING GOLF

BALL FLIGHT CONTROL

Control the golf ball, and you will play good golf. Once you have mastered the correct club path, you will quickly learn ball flight control. The golf learning sequence goes like this:

1. Learn the pre-swing fundamentals (grip, stance, posture).

2. Learn the mechanics of the short game and the full swing.

3. Learn ball flight control.

4. Apply your knowledge to the varying conditions of the golf course.

We're almost done! Now you are ready for step three.

There are two main factors which influence ball flight. They are the club path, and the club face angle. The **club path** is the direction in which you swing the club through impact, and can be either **inside-out** or **outside-in**. The **club face angle** is the direction in which a perpendicular line from the club face points at impact, and can be **open**, **closed**, or **square**. Let me explain the path first.

Stand behind the ball and look down the target line. To the left of the target line is inside, and to the right is outside. The opposite is true for left handers. When you take your stance to the ball, you stand to the left of, or inside, the target line. Right? Because you are holding a long stick in your hands, the club head must move inside the target line as you swing the club back. Therefore, the club should return to the ball from **inside** the target line, **out** to the target line. That's called an **inside-out** approach to the ball. Make sense? Everything you have learned so far has been designed to teach you to swing inside-out. Understand that not only are *you* designed to swing inside-out, so too is the golf club, that's why there is a lie angle. Forget any ideas of swinging the club straight back and through toward the target on a full swing, you can't possibly do it. Trying to do so can only make the club *and* your body work against you.

The **outside-in** approach to the ball is woefully common to amateur golfers. Due to a number of possible swing flaws, many golfers have the club head approaching the ball from outside (right of) the target line and then across the line to the left. This approach to the ball can cause big problems in your golf game. The dreaded slice, shots pulled left of the target, deep divots, pop-ups, and loss of power are common to this club path. If you have followed my instructions, you have nothing to worry about.

You are rapidly approaching the stage where you can finally use ball flight as feedback to evaluate your swing. Knowing your ball flight laws makes it easy to adjust your swing (which you should not have to do very much) and the club face angle, to control the ball.

Here's how it goes:

> **BALL FLIGHT LAW #1**
> **Initial direction is a function of the CLUB PATH.**

When you make contact with the ball, the ball compresses against the club face. This compression allows the ball to "stick to" the club face and pick up the direction in which the club head is traveling during the time of compression. The direction of the club head is called the **club path**. The **line of compression**, refers to the direction in which the club head travels while the ball is compressed against it. The line of compression (which is a fancy way of saying the club path), then, determines the direction in which the ball starts out, immediately after leaving the club face.

> **BALL FLIGHT LAW #2**
> **Curvature is a function of the CLUB FACE.**

The curve on a golf shot is caused by spin applied to the ball by the **club face**. Your club face can be **square** (straight to the target), **open** (to the right), or **closed** (to the left). The only way the ball can curve to the right is if the club face is aimed to the right at impact. Conversely, the only way the ball can curve to the left is if the club face is aimed to the left.

Note: These ball flight laws are not absolute, but they are extremely useful in learning to control your golf shots. If the **club face** is way off line, the ball will not have a chance to compress against it, and the ball will just slide off, making the first law non-applicable. However, if your grip is correct and you avoid the "death grip," your club face should be pretty close. As well, if the **club path** is way off, you can add curvature to the shot. I tell my students to ignore the really strange looking shots rather than try to "fix" them. You can't fix the bad shots. It's too late. Rehearse your good swing, and try again.

CHAPTER 6 — PRACTICING GOLF — 137

BALL FLIGHT LAWS QUIZ

1. What is the main determinant of the ball's **initial flight**?

2. What is the main determinant of the ball's **curvature**?

3. Ball starts left of the target and curves to the left. Was the **club path** inside-out, or outside in?

4. Ball starts right of the target and curves hard to the left. Was the **club face angle** open, closed, or square?

5. Ball starts left of the target and curves right. What was the **path**? What was the **face angle**?

6. Ball starts right of the target and draws to the target. What was the **path**? What was the **face angle**?

7. Club face square to path. Does the ball slice, draw, or go straight?

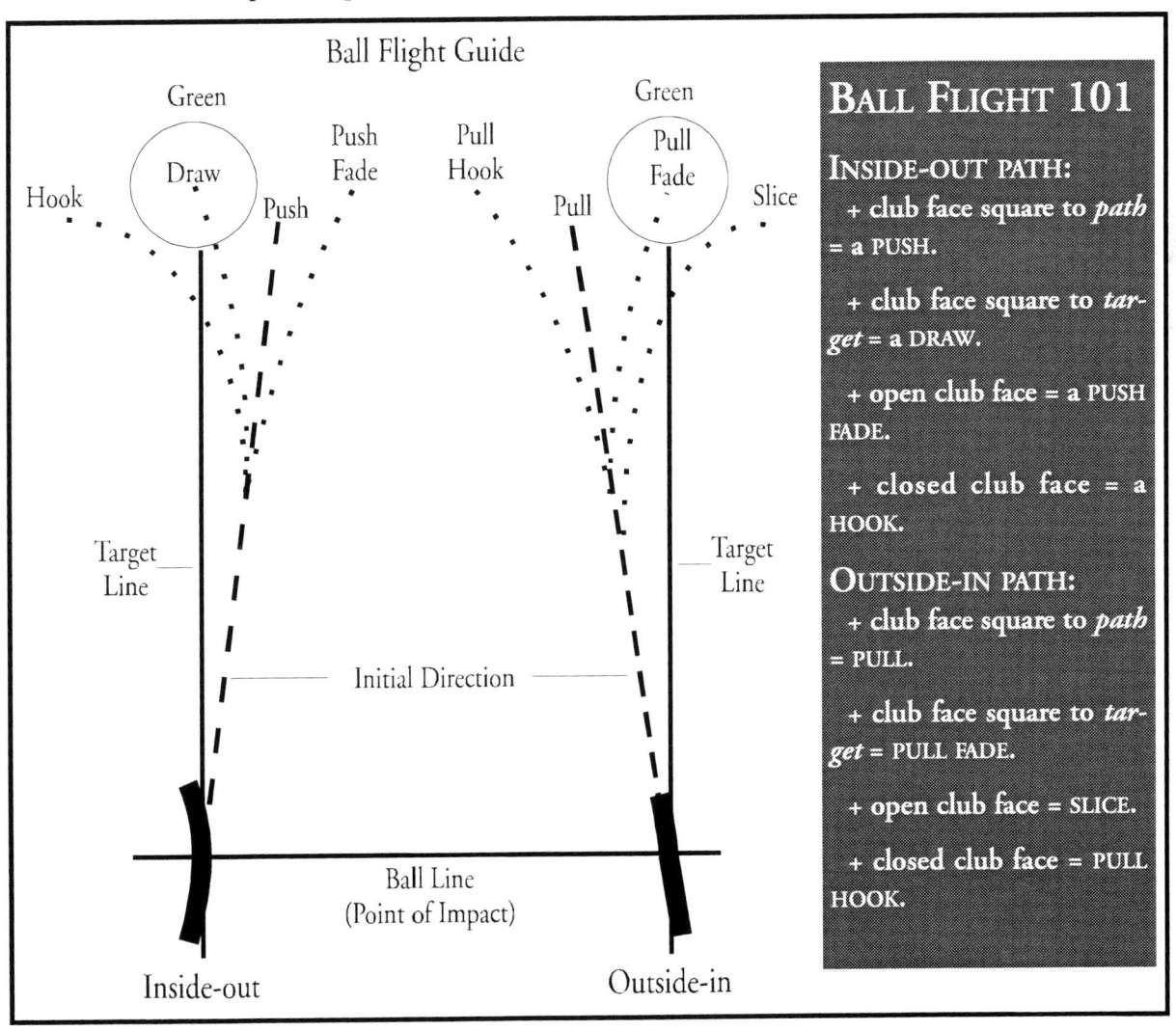

Ball Flight Guide

Left side (Inside-out): Hook, Draw (Green), Push, Push Fade
Right side (Outside-in): Pull Hook, Pull, Pull Fade (Green), Slice

Target Line — Initial Direction — Ball Line (Point of Impact)

BALL FLIGHT 101

INSIDE-OUT PATH:
+ club face square to *path* = a PUSH.
+ club face square to *target* = a DRAW.
+ open club face = a PUSH FADE.
+ closed club face = a HOOK.

OUTSIDE-IN PATH:
+ club face square to *path* = PULL.
+ club face square to *target* = PULL FADE.
+ open club face = SLICE.
+ closed club face = PULL HOOK.

OK, here are the answers. Again, ball flight is pretty basic. The ball goes where you hit it. 1, Club Path. 2, Club Face. 3, Outside in. 4, Closed. 5, Outside in path, Open club face. 6, Inside-out path, Square club face; great shot! 7, Straight.

Just understanding what makes the ball do what it does can really improve your golf game. When you understand what makes things happen, you can more readily make changes which will create the desired ball flight.

When you practice your ball flight control, make certain that you have an alignment club down on the ground so that you take the variable of alignment out of the following equation:

> **BALL FLIGHT = ALIGNMENT + CLUB PATH + CLUB FACE ANGLE**

You will do best to make alignment a given so that you can concentrate only on the path and the face angle.

You will do even better if you can make both alignment *and* club path given. That's what all the full swing instruction was for.

When you start the forward swing with the back and down move, the club will approach the ball from the inside just as it should. Therefore, your golf ball should start out slightly to the right of the target. Hopefully, the inside-out path is a given in our ball flight equation so that the only variable remaining is the club face angle. Let me state that another way: Before you can really learn how to bring the club face into impact squarely, you *need* both alignment and club path under control.

The ball flight goal for now is to create a right to left shaped curve, called a draw. A **draw** is the natural ball flight for the inside-out club path. Line up to the target, and try to hit the ball five yards to the right of it. Carefully watch where it goes. Do not judge the shot as either bad or good, just note where the ball started and adjust your path appropriately on the next shot. Keep your ball flight laws in mind. If the ball starts out immediately to the left of where you are aligned, your path was outside-in. Check your start down. Make sure that you start the forward swing by extending your right arm back and down. Feel that you are swinging the club a little to the right of the target. If the ball starts out slightly to the right of the target, your path was inside-out: That's what we want. Extend your energy slightly to the right of the target on the forward swing. If you have trouble getting the ball started in the right direction, fool yourself into the correct path by aiming at the actual target, but swinging the club 10, 20, or more yards to the right. It's surprising how strange the correct path can feel.

Next, watch how the ball curves. If the ball curves to the right (a slice), the club face was open at impact. If the ball curves to the left significantly (a hook), the club face was closed at impact. The more severe the curve, the more significantly the club face was open or closed. A "draw" is a mini-hook, and a "fade" is a mini-slice. What you need now is to educate your hands so that you can make the ball do whatever you want.

Educated Hands

To change your ball flight, first make sure that your club path is inside-out, and then work on either closing the club face a little more, or opening it a little more at impact. I call this process "educating your hands," and you will continually improve this skill as long as you play golf. Hand education deals with your ability to control the club face at impact. **You must have a consistent club path before you undertake educating your hands.** Different paths require different face angles to get the ball to the same target. If your path is inconsistent, it is difficult to educate your hands to perform consistently.

There is no substitute for educated hands. You can make up for a pretty unorthodox swing with good hands. There has *never* been a great player who didn't have great hands.

Continue to educate your hands by adjusting the club face position at impact. Try opening the club face on purpose and then try closing it. Try to hit big hooks to the left by over-rotating the club face way closed, and then make the ball slice to the right by under-rotating, leaving the face open. Then learn to work the hook down to a five yard draw. Hit and adjust and hit and adjust and have lots of fun. Forget about trying to hit the ball straight. The level of precision required to hit the ball straight is phenomenal. Even the great Ben Hogan said that if he ever hit a ball straight, it was an accident.

The loft on short irons imparts more backspin than sidespin to the ball, which straightens out the ball flight. You won't see too much curvature until you get to the 7 Iron. As you progress through the longer clubs on your way to the driver, you will notice increased curvature due to less backspin, and more side spin. Many people think they swing differently with short irons than long irons and woods, because the ball flies straighter with the shorter clubs. The fact is, you can get away with swing flaws with short irons, but the long clubs tell the truth about the quality of your swing. For now, do the majority of your practicing with a 7 or 6 Iron so that you can see curvature.

Another way to check your club path is to look at the direction of your divot, if you take one. The **divot** (the little patch of earth you remove after contact), should **not** go to the left of the target line. A divot that goes straight, or a little to the right is fine.

Here's an example of how I want you to practice. You hit a shot and the ball goes left of the target. Say to yourself, "Hmm, cool. More to the right please," and hit the next shot farther to the right. It's that easy. Keep adjusting your path and club face angle until you get the desired result. Remember that you may have to *feel* like you are swinging the club far right of the target to get the ball to go where you want. You may have to *feel* that you are rotating the club face too much and too soon to get the correct spin on the ball. That's OK. Adjust, adjust, adjust.

How to Practice Golf

Most people focus only on their full swing when they practice. Not only do most average golfers skip short game practice completely, but they usually spend most of their time practicing with the driver, which hurts their game more than anything. If you learn anything from this section of the book, let it be this: You must divide your practice time between short game and full swing practice. Actually, you should spend two thirds of your time on short game for maximum improvement, because two-thirds of the strokes you take in a round of golf will be either putts, chips, or pitches.

There are two modes of golf practice: Golf Swing mode, and Target Golf mode. These two modes are on absolute opposite sides of the golf spectrum, and you must discipline yourself to work in only one mode at a time. A good practice session, however, will include both modes of practice.

When you are in Golf Swing mode, you will work on and evaluate mechanics only. **While working on mechanics, *ignore both contact and ball flight*.** As you've already heard, if you *really* want to learn fast, slow everything down and use some sort of feedback mechanism so that you know you are practicing correctly. Do your drills. Do your late speed drill until you graduate to full speed. Practice with full attention and intention: Know exactly what you are working on and practice precisely. Constantly remind yourself of what your intentions are, and attend to your intentions.

When you swing the club, don't just swing it around. *Feel* the club in your hands. Concentrate on increasing your awareness of the club head. Turn your head and watch the club move. Try to bridge the gap between what you **see** the club doing and what you **feel** it is doing.

In the beginning of your golf education, spend seventy-five percent of your time on drills to learn your mechanics. As your mechanics improve, gradually lower that percentage until you spend only about twenty-five percent of your practice time drilling. After you've put in your time drilling, go on to ball flight control practice, which I have included under Golf Swing practice, although it is the link between the two modes.

In ball flight control practice, I want you to work on your **club path** and **face angle** to create a draw. Educate your hands. You can teach yourself to create any kind of shot you want. You will eventually need to be able to make the ball curve in both directions, so go ahead and play around. See what you can make the ball do and have fun. It's really neat to be able to control the ball, and when you can control the ball a little, you are ready for Target Golf.

When you practice, you must be certain that your alignment is correct. Alignment is critical. You must know where you are lined up to evaluate your ball flight.

Help yourself align to the target by laying down a club parallel to the target line. You don't have to stand so that your feet touch the club, but you should be within three or four inches of it. Imagine train tracks running to the target: your feet go on one track and the ball goes on the other. Always practice with alignment clubs. Alignment is one of the easiest fundamentals to get right, and *the* easiest to get wrong. Misalignment is the single greatest cause of poor shots once you get your swing down.

OK, good alignment is now a given, and you can now work on getting the ball to the target by going through your pre-shot routine *every time you try to hit a ball to a target, for the rest of your life!!!*

When in Target Golf mode, use your pre-shot routine, and concentrate only on the target. It's pretty simple, folks. Practice picking out a target and concentrating solely on the target while you swing, just as you will need to do on the golf course. Target Golf requires that you trust your swing, whatever state of repair it is in, regardless of whether you still have things to work on. Trusting your swing takes practice, too, so make sure that you spend ample practice time just focusing on the target and trusting your swing.

Target Golf practice is just like playing a round of golf on the range. Practicing in this way will greatly help you bring your best golf to the golf course. I'm sure you know many people who are what I call "Range Pros." They look great on the range, but fall apart on the course. These folks just need to change the way they practice to greatly improve their game. The Pre-Shot routine is the key to getting your mind focused on the task at hand, so that you give yourself the opportunity to play your best golf. That's all you can ask of yourself.

> ## The Adjusted Target
>
> I have found it astoundingly successful to have my students aim and align to their *actual* target, and then pick out an *adjusted*, or secondary, target to which they will swing the club. To get the ball to the actual target, the adjusted target very often needs to be well right of the actual, because feel is not real. Sometimes you have to fool yourself into swinging toward the actual target by *feeling* like you are swinging way right of it. Wow, does this idea work wonders for many students!

Pre-Shot Routine, Part 2

We have already discussed the Pre-Shot Routine, but I'd like to get a little deeper into it now. As I have said, before you hit a golf ball, you will want to preprogram your brain for success by going through the three steps that make up your pre-shot routine.

First, SEE the shot you are trying to hit. Visualize the flight of the ball, including how the wind will affect the shot and the way the ball will bounce and roll to the target, or into the hole.

Second, FEEL the swing which makes the ball go to the target. This stage is up to you. Sometimes you will need several rehearsal swings to get the right feel, and sometimes you may need only one. Do not get into the habit of taking the same number of swings each time just to make your routine the same each time. Take rehearsal swings until your brain tells you you're ready. Remember the difference between practice and rehearsal.

Third, look at your target to lock it in mind, then look back to the ball and then DO IT. If you want the ball to go to the target, you must commit yourself to the shot you are on by swinging with only the target in mind. That goes for every shot you hit. Your mind needs to be focused on one thing in order to function at its potential. What better object to focus on than the target? When you have swing thoughts in your mind, you are not focused on the target. Save swing thoughts for Golf Swing practice. When you have a target to get to, you need to trust what you've trained and swing freely.

After you hit the shot, smile if you've hit it well. Tell yourself "That's a goodie!" If you've gotten an undesirable result, immediately make a perfect practice swing and tell yourself "That's the right swing!" When you make this *review swing*, imagine the ball flying right where you wanted it to go. Get a positive charge from your review swing just as if you had actually hit the shot that way. Your brain stores whatever you give more emotion to, so give emotion only to results you want to store. Don't let undesirable results bug you. That only makes them stand out in your mind. You don't want that, do you?

It's like programming a computer. Your pre-shot routine is programming your brain for success. Your post-shot (review) swing is a way of reprogramming yourself after a less desirable outcome. It helps to put a bad swing out of your mind fast, and replace it with a good swing. For every shot, do the Three R's; Rehearsal Swing, Real Swing, and Review swing.

CHAPTER 6   PRACTICING GOLF   143

RECOMMENDED PRACTICE ROUTINE

Here is a great daily practice routine for you to follow:

You may not practice every day, but whenever you get to practice, do it this way, and you'll improve fast. Get to the putting green and begin your putting drills. Start with ten in a row from two feet and then ten more from three feet. Do the Around the World drill from three feet. Do the North, South, East and West drill from three paces. Do the Twenty Footer drill, and then do the Three Ball drill and the Twelve Ball drill until you feel good about your distance control. Play games against a friend if you can.

Move onto chipping, starting with your sand wedge, and finish chipping practice with the Up and Down Game. Don't go on until you get at least five up and down. As you improve, set the number higher. You don't have to get them all in a row, by the way.

Next, warm up your full swing with a pitching game I call Leap Frog. With a sand wedge, hit a five yard pitch shot, and note where the ball comes to a stop. Try to land the next ball on top of the previous one. Continue the process until you reach full swing. Not only will you have a slow and thorough warm-up, but you will also have practiced one of the most important scoring skills you need.

After you finish warming up, go to the full swing with your 7 Iron, and do the late speed drill, starting at 50 yds and progressing by 25 yds until you reach full speed. Make sure you *graduate* to full speed, don't skip right to it. Once that's done, it's time to forget about mechanics and send the ball to a target.

Start with sand wedge and work on accuracy. Do not use another club until you are satisfied with your wedge. Make a goal of so many balls on the green or within a certain area before you change clubs, and work your way up through your set. A goal of just two or three good shots is fine for now. You can increase that number as you improve. Spend most of your time *hitting golf shots* with your 6, 7, 8, and 9 Irons, and your wedges. Spend a little time on long irons, but don't overdo it. Of all the long clubs, spend the most time with your 3 Wood, because it will probably be your most reliable club when you really need to get the ball in play off the tee.

Long irons and the driver may make you get real fast with your tempo if you try to press for distance. You do not need to swing any harder to hit the ball farther with longer clubs. Your clubs are designed with different length shafts and different lofts to automatically hit the ball different distances. The only thing you need to change is how far apart you set your feet at address. Your clubs will even tell you how far to stand from the ball. You just have to let your arms hang down loosely at address. Let the clubs do the work.

Find a friend at the range and play closest to the pin contests to make practice more fun and meaningful. Play golf on the range. Imagine the holes at your golf course, and play a few holes from tee to green. Go through your routine and hit a drive. Switch clubs and hit an iron. Imagine long holes and short holes. Realize that in golf, you will seldom get to use the same club twice in a row. You need to practice switching between clubs. Use your imagination. Do anything you can to make practice more realistic and more fun.

Remember, this is supposed to be fun. Whenever you have a club in your hands, it is better to think that you are playing, not working.

THE ART OF PRACTICING

Note the two alignment clubs on the ground by my feet. Imagine a set of train tracks going toward the target. Your feet go on the inside rail, and the ball goes on the outside rail. Make certain that you are properly aligned to the target, and then can you work on your ball flight control.

Avoid the "Fix it" Mentality

Don't try to fix the last swing. It's too late, not to mention unnecessary. Do you know what your good swing is? If you do, you never need to fix anything. You just have to replace your errant swings with your good swing and carry on.

A lot of golfers waste a lot of mental energy trying to figure out what's wrong with their swing during a round of golf. The fact is, you have no way of knowing whether you are actually making a mechanical error, or aligning poorly, or simply experiencing brain interference rather than focusing on the target. Swings don't break down. Something we do in the process of swinging is where we go wrong.

Using Video Tape

As you know, I highly recommend using good feedback, and video is best. When shooting the target line view, set the camera so that it is parallel to the target line, and your right shoulder is in the center of the lens. If you don't get the camera at parallel to the target line, your view will be inaccurate. For the facing view, make sure the camera lens is perpendicular to the target line, and you are centered in the lens. The other angles shown in this book are good for illustration, but you'll need to use the facing view, and the target line view for yourself. I'll usually tape three or four swings, then look at them, and then go back and tape three or four more with the necessary adjustment. Try to work only on one thing at a time, it's much easier on your brain.

Tempo

A golf instruction book would be incomplete without some mention of tempo. Tempo can be defined loosely as the quickness of your swing. Tempo can be related to your speech. Someone who talks fast has a quick tempo and so on. Your tempo is in reference to your pre-shot routine, overall swing, and more particularly, the transition from backswing to forward swing.

I would like to say that while there are probably as many different tempos as there are different golfers, it is best to have a relaxed, unhurried tempo. Even your approach to the ball should be leisurely. You want to have an overall attitude of calm confidence when you hit the ball, and I assure you that rushing into the shot is no way to cultivate that attitude.

Practicing your swing slowly, as you have done before and will hopefully continue to do, is a very good exercise not only to learn the swing, but also to help your tempo. I still hit balls in slow motion and half speed just to keep my tempo from getting too quick. I try to see how short I can hit a full swing driver while making solid contact.

It is true that someone who talks fast, walks fast, eats fast, etc. will probably have a quicker tempo than someone who naturally does the same things slowly, but I maintain that there should be no hurry to get the shot over with. Let me put it this way. I rarely see anyone swing too slowly, but I regularly see people swing too fast.

Good tempo is probably most needed at the transition from backswing to forward swing. The transition should almost feel to be in slow motion, although we begin accelerating the club head immediately. I think of it more like an airplane taking off rather than like a gun shot. It is a smooth start forward and constant acceleration that we are after, not one quick burst of speed.

When I feel that my tempo is getting too quick, I will hit one shot in slow motion, the next at half speed and then next at full speed. Then I will start over. Usually, I will immediately get my swing back under control by doing so.

There are some wonderful players whose tempo you would do well to imitate. Davis Love swings so slowly you'd think he's never going to get to the ball yet he's one of the longest hitters on the tour. Nick Faldo, Phil Mickelson, Fred Couples and Ernie Els are also great examples.

7
DIFFERENT LIES

The "lie" refers to how your ball sits on the ground (or elsewhere). One of the inevitabilities of golf is that your ball will come to rest in a very different lie than you will find on the driving range. To become a golfer, you need to learn how to handle these somewhat more challenging shots, so practice them out on the course whenever you have a chance. Different lies include downhill, uphill, sidehill (below your feet or above your feet), in rough or on a bare spot, and sand shots. There's not really much to them, they may be more challenging, but not much. And, believe it or not, sand play is easy!

DOWNHILL

When your ball comes to rest on a downhill slope, you must realize that the ball is going to fly lower than normal and tend to curve to the right.

Take several practice swings in as similar a lie as your ball is in (to the side of the ball or in front or behind it) and note where the club hits the ground. These practice swings will give you an idea of where to position the ball in your stance (probably a little back).

When addressing the ball, get as comfortable with the lie as possible. Don't fight the slope, allow your weight to be more on your front foot at address, and try to feel as solid and balanced as possible. Don't hit the ball until you are quite comfortable with your stance.

This shot will probably want to curve to the right on you, so you may want to aim a little left to allow for the curve. The ball will also fly lower and "hotter" than normal, so you may want to use a more lofted club than the one you'd normally hit. If it's a normal 8 Iron shot, you may want to hit a 9 Iron instead.

Uphill

Take your practice swings and get comfortable as before. Move the ball a little forward in your stance to avoid digging into the hill, and try to sweep the ball up the slope. Once again, don't fight the slope, let it tell your body how to relax into address.

This ball will fly higher and shorter than normal, so you should use a less lofted club to cover the required distance. The ball will also tend to curve to the left on you. Adjust your aim appropriately.

BALANCE IS THE KEY
Get as comfortable as you can on all "different lies," and swing well within yourself to maintain balance through the swing.

SIDEHILL, ABOVE YOUR FEET

Choke down on the grip a little or a lot, relative to how much the ball is above your feet. Place the ball in the middle of your stance. Take some practice swings and get comfortable. Sound familiar? This ball will want to curve to the left (hook) on you. The more severe the lie, the more the ball will hook. Aim accordingly to the right.

SIDEHILL, BELOW YOUR FEET

Again, take some practice swings and get comfortable. Place ball position in the middle and get ready for the ball to curve to the right on you. The more severe the lie, the more the ball will fade on you, so adjust your aim.

Rough

There is deep rough and short rough, and the ball can be buried or sitting up. You have to be able to "read the rough" as you would a putting green.

In deep rough, the club will tend to get caught in the grass, forcing the club face to close, very often sending the ball left of the target. If the ball is sitting down, buried in thick grass, use a more lofted club, perhaps only enough club to get safely back into the fairway and avoid more trouble, and allow for the ball to go left. You may want to hold on more tightly through impact, to keep the club face from closing down severely.

Heavy Rough

In short rough, the ball may fly farther than normal due to grass getting between the ball and club face. You will hear the term "flyer lie" often on TV golf telecasts. The flyer is hard to predict, because the ball seems to "jump" out of light rough sometimes. Grass between the ball and the club face at impact results in less backspin and less sidespin. Less backspin means the ball will tend to roll more than usual once it hits the ground. You will want to land the ball short of the target and let it run up. Less sidespin means the ball will also fly quite straight, so don't expect much curve. You are best off to figure out whether you'd rather be short or long, and then play accordingly. Take a look at the target and determine where the trouble is. Choose the club which will be sure to avoid the worst trouble.

Flyer Lie

TIGHT LIES

A "tight" lie (aka. "bare" lie) has little or no grass around or beneath the ball. The ball will fly lower and "hotter" than normal, so use one less club. No other adjustment need be done other than possibly moving the ball position a little farther back in your stance. Don't let this lie bother you. It is no more difficult than a ball sitting on good fairway grass. You always hit the ball first anyway, right?

IN A DIVOT

As far as I'm concerned, this should never happen, at least not when your ball is in the fairway. I think the rules of golf should allow relief for such a lie. You shouldn't have to pay for some person's lack of consideration. So, if you are not playing in a tournament, move the ball out of the divot. If you want, or need, to leave the ball in the divot, just play the ball back in your stance and get ready for a heavy thud at impact. This ball will fly very low, and probably shorter than normal.

Sand Play

As I've said before, sand play is surprisingly easy, once you learn how it's done. There are two types of bunkers, green-side and fairway, and they require completely different techniques. In a green-side bunker, you will contact the sand rather than the ball, and let the sand "push" the ball out. In a fairway bunker, you must contact the ball first, as usual. We'll start with green-side bunkers.

There are two different shots used to get the ball out of green-side bunkers. For good lies, where the ball is sitting nicely on top of the sand, you will slide the club under the ball with a shallow divot: a "slider." When the ball is buried in the sand, in a foot print, or in a depression, you will blast the ball out with a deep divot: an "explosion."

The Slider

For the Slider, position the ball just slightly to the left of center. Open the club face to make use of your sand wedge's "bounce" sole, which is designed to cut through the sand without digging. Align your stance to the left of the target to allow for the open club face, splitting the difference between how far right you aim the club face. For instance, if you aim the club face five yards right of the target, align your stance five yards to the left. The net effect is that the ball will go straight to the target. Dig your feet down into the sand to give yourself firm footing. Put your weight mainly on your left foot. Make a normal swing and try to enter the sand three inches behind the ball. Make sure you swing through impact. Don't let the sand stop you from finishing your swing. If you find that your club stops at impact, you are probably going too deep and taking too much sand.

To vary distances, shorten or lengthen your swing, and possibly vary the speed of your swing. For longer shots use a longer backswing, and do just the opposite for shorter shots.

You may want to start out with a simple Three Quarter Backswing at first, as you get used to hitting the sand instead of the ball.

Remember: You don't even have to hit the ball. How hard could this be?!

Getting out of bunkers is easy, it just takes a little understanding of the technique involved, and some practice. The main objective of your practice is to get used to opening the club face and to work out how deep into the sand you need the club to go to get the ball out. Getting the ball close requires a lot of practice, but getting out is easy.

To summarize:

- Ball position **left** of center.
- Align your stance **left** of the target.
- Set your weight firmly on your **left** foot.

Remember: **Triple Left Setup**

Then:
- Dig your feet in.
- Accelerate through the sand.
- Swing to a full finish.

DRILL

THE RAKE LINE

This drill does not require a ball. In a practice bunker, rake a straight line that is about ten feet long. Then use the butt end of the rake to draw a small line, centered along the length of your big (raked) line. Start at the left end of the line, and swing at the small line. Try to remove equal amounts of sand from both sides of the line, but keep your divot within the big line.

Experiment with short and long swings, with the club face open and closed, and with the depth of the divot you take to get a feel for how to change the distance you would hit a ball.

EASIEST PART OF THE GAME

Every other part of golf requires nearly perfect contact to hit good shots. Bunker shots allow you far more room for error. You must experiment to find how far behind the ball you need to hit, and how deep into the sand you have to swing, to hit good shots. Remember: You must accelerate through contact!

DRILL

WHERE TO ENTER THE SAND

After you become comfortable with taking sand, put a ball down and with the club head, draw a line in the sand, three inches behind the ball. Try to hit the line first on your way under the ball. If you feel that contact with the sand is stopping you from finishing your swing, you are probably hitting too low beneath the ball, taking too much of a divot. I know it may sound a little too simple, but it really is just a matter of adjusting your swing, either lower or higher, until you find what works.

A DAY AT THE BEACH

Note my address position, particularly the club face angle. My stance is left of the target, and my club face is well right of (open to) the target. Once you are comfortable with sand play setup, get into a bunker and hit a bunch of shots. Play in the sand. You'll improve very quickly.

The Explosion

When the ball is sitting down in the sand, buried, or very close to the front edge of a bunker, you will need to blast it out forcefully. The setup is the same as for the slider, but do not open the club face. Square the club face, and it will dig into the sand for you. Note the difference in ball position and club face angle at address between the Explosion and the Slider, it's important!

Don't be afraid to swing down forcefully, you are going to have to move a lot of sand to get the sand to push the ball out of the bunker. And don't be surprised if you are unable to finish your swing.

Practice bunker shots from every kind of lie you can think of. Put the ball in a foot print, a divot, step on it, throw it into the sand so that it looks like a "fried egg," and see what happens, you'll be way ahead of the game.

Play at Learning

It's easy to turn golf into work. Don't do it. Choose to have fun, and choose to approach learning the game just as a child would. You'll learn faster, and golf won't be an additional source of frustration for you (you probably have enough already).

Fairway Bunkers

Fairway bunkers require a different strategy, but are not really all that difficult to play from if you assess the lie properly and play accordingly. The first job is to check the lie of the ball. Is it sitting up on top of the sand, or is sand behind the ball? Sand behind the ball will make it impossible to contact the ball first. Is the edge of the bunker much higher than the ball? And how close to the edge is the ball?

If the edge of the bunker is high, or the ball is sitting down, take out a sand wedge and hit a normal sand shot out safely into play. If you have a good lie and don't have to worry about getting the ball up and over the edge, here's what to do.

- Play the ball just left of center.
- Dig your feet in just a little.
- Make your feet and legs feel dead.
- Take the club back slowly and try to hit the ball first.

Remember: You always hit the ball first anyway, so this is no big deal. The ball may tend to fade on you, so aim a little left. Also use a longer club than you would normally use for that distance and swing easier so that you can keep your balance better.

Play Smart

Play conservatively on fairway bunker shots, and avoid trying to pull off a spectacular shot, because if the club hits the sand first, the ball won't go very far at all. Be aggressive with your swing, but choose your target wisely. By the way, that's a good strategy for the entire game.

8
Playing Golf

Well, here we are, ready to play. By now, you have considerable high-quality practice time behind you on all aspects of the game, and have much more than just an understanding of the mechanics of the short game and full swing. You are now ready to apply your knowledge.

You should be reasonably confident in your ability to send the ball near the target before you attempt a busy, full size golf course. I don't mean to say that you should be shooting par already, but if you are hitting the ball sideways, you are not ready for the golf course. That may sound harsh, but it's true. If you go on the course before you are ready, you're going to find out how difficult this game can be. I'm trying to help you avoid that.

Before you do golf your ball, however, there are a few things you should know. This chapter will give you everything you need to know about *playing* golf. We'll start with etiquette, and then move on to playing the game.

Etiquette

I'm no Emily Post, but there are a few things you need to know before you go on the course. Not knowing golf's protocol can be quite embarrassing if you are playing with other golfers, especially golfers you don't know. All it takes to look like you belong on a golf course is a little awareness and consideration.

What to wear

Collared shirts and pants or Bermuda shorts. Golf shoes really help, and give you much more support than running shoes or tennis shoes. No T-shirts or denims. Women may wear skirts, shorts or pants and golf shirts. Some clubs allow women to wear sleeveless shirts. Golf is an elegant game, and we should keep it that way. I wouldn't mind a bit if we still played in our Sunday best. Bring sun screen. You are going to bake out there.

Your tee time

Call the pro shop to get a tee time, and don't be surprised if you are asked to give a credit card number over the phone to secure it, if you are going to play a busy course. Most courses allow you to make a tee time up to one week in advance, and some don't take walk-ons, so give a call to be sure you can play.

You are supposed to be teeing off at your tee time, not just getting to the course, so arrive at the course at least 15 minutes before your tee time. Get there an hour early if you can. An hour will give you time to stretch a little, hit a few range balls, and get in a little putting and chipping practice. This warm-up time is a whole lot better for your score than using the first few holes to warm-up.

Where to stand

When others in your group are playing, you should stand so that you face the golfer whenever possible. When others are teeing off, you may stand behind them so that you have their ball and the target in line to help them see their ball. I often have a player in my group watch my shot this way when I'm playing into the sun. Some players don't like anyone to stand behind them at all, so be wary.

Other than on the tee shot, you may stand slightly ahead and to the side of other players, but not so much that you distract them, or put yourself in danger of a stray shot. The best way to find out what distracts people is to ask. You want to get to your ball as quickly as possible, but you don't want to bother the others in your group. I sometimes see all the players in a group waiting behind one player while he hits, and then they all move to the next ball and so on, in a really slow parade around the golf course. Carts can actually slow down play when players wait at each others ball. Drop your rider off at his/her ball and then go to your ball. Don't wait. The key to keeping play moving is to be as near your ball as possible, so that you may play your shot as soon as it is your turn.

Two big No, No's are walking and talking while others are hitting. When a player takes his/her stance, there should be no talking and no distracting movement.

Who goes first?

The order of play for the first shot is decided on the first tee by flipping a coin, spinning a tee to see who it points to, or simply by asking who wants to go first. Unless you are in a tournament, you don't have to be formal.

After the first hole, the player with the lowest score on the previous hole will have the "honor" and will play his/her tee shot first, followed by the player with the next lowest score and so on.

On the rest of the course, including the putting green, the player who is farthest from the hole will play first. When players make the same score, the order from the previous hole is kept.

When in a group where players are playing from different sets of tees, allow those on the more rearward tees to play first.

Carts

First of all, don't take a cart if you can avoid it. The game is meant for walking and enjoying the surroundings. Golf, for many, has turned into a race, with golfers speeding from shot to shot, completely missing the beauty of the sport.

If you are going to use a cart, please obey the signs up on the course that tell you where to drive. There are good reasons why the course superintendent puts up cart travel signs. You will damage either yourself, or the course if you don't follow these signs.

Always keep carts away from the greens. Don't park or drive where you think someone might have to chip or pitch from. If there are cart paths around the greens, use them. It's just consideration. How would you like it if your ball came to rest in a tire track near the green?

Slow Play

Slow play is not pretty, and not being a good golfer is not a good reason for being a slow player. Play slows down because players either are not ready to hit when their turn comes, or they spend too much time looking for balls.

Be ready when your turn comes by moving to your ball quickly and lining up your shot while the others in your group are hitting their shots, whenever possible. You don't want to walk too far in front of your group, because you don't want to distract them or get hit, but if you can get a little ahead, it will help. ***Be ready when it's your turn!***

This business of looking for balls on the golf course has gotten way out of hand. I know golf balls are expensive but they are not made of gold. If you have to look for a ball, make it quick, and if another group comes up behind you, either move it along, or let them play through.

Agree to play ready golf when you get on the first tee. Ready golf means exactly what you think. First one to their ball plays first.

Some people look for more than their own ball and really slow down play. We call these folks "ball hawks," and they have no place on the golf course, except when no one else is on it (i.e. just about never). Some ball hawks think it's OK to look for balls when they are not playing. They will come to the course and scour the high grass for balls while others are playing. This practice is wrong and should be disallowed totally. It is distracting to players and unsafe for the ball hawks.

When you lose a ball

You are going to lose a ball at some point in your career. You might lose a lot of them. When you hit a shot that you don't think you will find, and the ball did not go into a **water hazard**, the proper procedure is to play a **provisional ball**, as allowed in the rules. If you think you might have lost your tee shot, wait for the others to tee off, and then announce that you are going to play a provisional ball and do so.

If, after a brief search (two minutes, max.), you come up empty, play your provisional ball. You must count the original shot, add a penalty stroke, and resume counting your strokes as normal. The provisional ball option may be applied to balls lost from any position on the course, except for a ball lost in a water hazard.

A ball lost in a water hazard is different. You may *not* play a provisional ball in this case. You may reload from the tee, or drop another ball as near to the spot from which you played the previous ball and add a stroke penalty, (the only time you *should* do so is when the hazard is right in front of you).

Otherwise, you should drop a ball within two club lengths of where the ball last crossed the hazard's margin, and play from there with a one stroke penalty.

The Rules of Golf book is not really meant for the casual golfer to read and understand, but there is a book called *Golf Rules in Pictures* by the USGA (United Stated Golf Association) that is very worth reading.

On the putting green

The putting green is sacred ground. You must be careful not to walk on anyone's line to the hole. That may be the biggest No, No in golf. You may step over the line or walk around it to avoid the evil eye.

When your ball is close to anyone's line of putt, you should mark it with a coin or other small object. When your marker is directly in someone's way, you may move it one or more putter head lengths to the side, and then return it after they putt. When moving your marker, use a tree or some other object to move it toward so that you may accurately replace it.

When a player is a long distance from the hole, you may be asked to "attend" the flag stick (often called "tend"). You should stand as far from the hole as possible and so that your shadow does not cover the hole while you hold the flag stick, to mark the hole for the other player. Hold the flag, itself, so that it does not blow in the wind. After the ball is struck, pull out the flag stick so that the ball does not hit it. Then place the flag stick on the fringe, out of everyone's way.

MARKING A BALL

Place your bag near the green, but never on it, and out of the way of everyone's line of play. Preferably place it so that it is on your way to the next hole.

Try to line up your putts as much as you can while the others are putting so that you will be ready when it is your turn. However, do not move around while they are standing over the ball preparing to putt.

Please be careful when walking on the greens. Some people (inadvertently, I hope) drag their feet or twist their spikes in the green as they walk, and really damage the putting surface. Never run on the putting green.

Maintaining the course

True golfers keep the course in good condition for those behind them. Fix your divots in the fairways and on tees either by be replacing them, or filling them with sand/seed mix, depending on the preferred method at that course. Repair ball marks on the green and fringe by using a tee or ball mark repair tool. Pull back the pushed-up part, then lift around the indentation to make it more level. Finally, tap with the sole of your putter to even it off. Make it as flat as possible. You may even want to fix more than one just because you care. Rake your footprints and divots in bunkers. There is nothing more annoying than to hit your ball into a bunker and then find it in some jerk's footprint. Some clubs differ in their policy, but it is a good idea to place the rake in the bunker when you are through.

Sometimes you will see a little box at par three holes. This box is filled with a sand/seed mixture that should be used to fill in divots. Fill yours and another.

Playing through

You may find your group is holding up play and backing up the course. When there is no one on the hole in front of you, you are playing too slowly. When there is a hole open in front of you and there is a group right behind you on your heels, you should allow them to play through.

The same deal applies when you are being held up and there is a hole open in front of the group ahead of you. They should allow you to play through, but sometimes they don't for one reason or another. You may want to tactfully ask them *after* you find out for certain that there is a hole open ahead of them.

There really isn't much more to golf's etiquette than that. It's pretty much common sense and decency. Just be aware of the other people around (and not only those in your group), keep moving, and keep the course in the condition you want it to be in, and you'll be just fine. Oh, one more thing. Turn off your cellular phone and don't use it on the golf course. Better yet, don't even bring it with you.

You don't have to be embarrassed about how well you play, most people aren't much better than you anyway, but when you fail to observe the etiquette of the game, that's embarrassing.

Golf: The Mind Game

Finally, after all that, we come to what you really wanted to know: How to play golf.

You have learned the techniques of the full swing and the short game, and how to apply them to the conditions you find on the golf course. Now you are ready to use what you have learned to score on the course. Here, we will consider the real game: How to think on the course.

Everything you have learned so far has been easy. The difficult part of golf is between your ears. You need to put your brain in gear to give yourself the best possible chance to score well. There is a wealth of literature on the psychology of golf, and while I am no psychologist, I can tell you what I think are the basics of golf psychology.

Basically, you are in total control of what you think. Your job is simply to put your brain in the right place on every shot. Sounds easy. Actually, I could end this discussion right here, because there really is nothing more to the game. Missed shots are more a result of poor preparation for the shot than poor technique. If you want good results, concentrate on the shot you are about to hit (in the present), not on what just happened (in the past), or what might happen (in the future). You can't do anything about the shot you just hit, you can only give yourself the best possible chance of success on the shot you are faced with. The way to give yourself the best chance is to go through your routine every time and make sure that you commit to the shot you are hitting. As I have already said, you are committed to the shot only when you have nothing but the target in mind when you swing. Think of throwing a dart. You never think of how to throw it, you just look at the target and throw. Do the same on the golf course.

Some golfers work on their swing on the range and then go to the golf course and work on it some more. I appreciate the desire to improve their swing that these players have, but please understand that it is more important that you learn how to focus your attention solely on the target and trust your swing, although you may still need work on it. That's the real challenge of golf. Just watch the tour players. There are a lot of them who have less than perfect swings, but they still manage to shoot low scores.

The ability to commit to the shot at hand is the most important skill you will develop in your quest for lower scores. Let me tell you, it's hard to let go of those technical thoughts that run through your mind as you try to swing the club. You will have to practice it on the range. Don't just try to do it on the course. You need to *practice playing* (committing to the shot and trusting yourself) on the range. Think about it. If you focus your attention on swing mechanics, doesn't that automatically make it impossible to focus your attention on the target at the same time? Golf is a target game, and so you must focus on the target if you want the ball to go there. Train your golf swing at the range, and trust what you've trained as soon as you step on the course. And, of course, practice trusting your swing at the range too. The same applies to the short game, as well.

Realize that, no matter how good you get, you will always hit some strange looking golf shots. Don't try to fix those shots on the golf course. Just let them go. So many golfers try to fix their swing, only to have the wheels come completely off. The reason is that the more mechanical they become, the farther away their attention goes from the target. After you hit one of those weird ones, take a practice swing or two to remind yourself of what you had intended to do, accept the shot, and go on to the next. The secret of golf psychology is to force yourself to think properly. You must forget about the shot you just hit, in order to prepare yourself for the shot you are about to hit. Your pre-shot routine is designed to help you do just that, so stick to your pre-shot routine.

Whenever you hit a shot that is playable, count it as a good shot. Avoid perfectionism. You'll seldom see the best golfers in the world hit perfect shots. So when you hit a "good enough" shot, don't analyze why it didn't fly *exactly* as you had hoped. If you can find the ball after you've hit it, that's good enough. Go hit it again. Don't get too excited about bad shots. Thinking about the shot you just missed is living in the past, and does not help you hit the next shot at all.

My own experience playing golf has led to an important self-discovery. It seems as though there are key moments during a round of golf where I have to make a decision as to how I will react to a missed shot. Those times when I have allowed myself to get angry have often led to an overall negative attitude throughout the round. Although I have often been able to recover and play "good" golf, the times when I have chosen to get angry have often ruined my whole day, and that's just not good.

However, on the days when I have forced myself to accept missed shots and just moved on to the next shot, regardless of my score, I have *always* managed to have a good day. Thinking properly does not always mean that I play well, but at least the bad round doesn't come home with me.

The least I can say after a round where I have thought properly is that I gave myself the best chance to play well that I could. The best you can do is the best you can do, so don't panic.

Lower scores are not the only goal in golf, you know. Some people are happy just to be on the course and could care less what they shoot. These people may have the right idea. Playing golf just for the fun of it will loosen you up. You will hit more good shots if you don't have the self imposed pressure to hit every shot well. *Try* to hit every shot perfectly, but don't *expect* to.

Some of us work hard at the game and feel we deserve to play better. We get frustrated when we shoot higher scores than we are capable of, because we feel that we *should* play better. Chuck Hogan, one of the best golf coaches in the world and someone I admire greatly, used to wear a shirt that had the message, "Don't **Should** on Me" printed on it. I think I'm going to get one of those. We need to learn to give ourselves the best possible chance to score well, and be happy with that. Golf is difficult, unpredictable and can be maddening if you look at your results rather than at the *process* of golfing your ball.

The process of golfing requires that you focus your attention. Playing your best requires a good pre-shot routine, confidence, commitment, and composure.

Pre-shot routine

Your pre-shot routine is, when it comes to actually playing golf, the most important weapon in your bag. Although we have discussed it many times before, I feel that it is worth mentioning yet again. Your routine puts your mind in focus for the task at hand.

1 See it

2 Feel it

3 Do it

LISTEN. We've been over this before: if you want to play well, do not put Step Three ahead of Step One and Step Two.

Before you get to Step One, you must go through a situation assessment in which you will check your lie, the wind, locate trouble and use these factors to help you select a target. Begin this assessment as you walk to the ball, and finalize it when you get there.

Step One: See it

Visualization is a vitally important skill which you can and should improve with practice. See the flight you wish ball to take, including what effect the wind will have on it, and see the way it will bounce and roll to the target. Visualizing helps the mind and body work together. You may do this several times before you actually swing, and the shot you visualize may help you to choose which club to hit.

This process need not take more than a few seconds, and it will pay big dividends as you focus more clearly on the target and make better shots because of that.

You should visualize all shots from full shots to the shortest putts. It's like playing in your head a movie of your shot before you swing. The great Jack Nicklaus said that he never hit a shot without visualizing first, not even in practice.

If you find it difficult to see the ball flying high against the sky at first, you may want to see a road in the sky or on the green or anything you can think of. Some players use a train on a track for putting and see the train fall into the hole. Anything that locks you onto the target will work.

Step Two: Feel it

Step Two is simple. Feel the swing you need to make to create the shot you have visualized.

Sometimes you will need only one swing to feel it, and sometimes you will need more. The point is, do not hit the ball until you are confident that you are ready. Seeing the shot will automatically trigger a muscular response, feeling the right swing will make it absolutely clear, and then you only have to fix the target in your mind and swing. SEE it and FEEL it until your brain tells you you're ready. *Rehearse* the shot, don't *practice* your mechanics.

Step Three: Do it

Step Three is what many players do as Step One. The problem is that they have done little to give themselves the best possible chance to hit a good shot.

Step Three consists of locking the target in your mind and holding it there while you swing the club. After you address the ball and go through your waggles, look one last time at the target and then slowly move your eyes to the ball. Pause briefly, and then send your energy to the target you have in your mind's eye. Again, this process goes for all shots, from driving to putting. Remember to "Target Lock."

After the shot, rate the quality of your focus on the target on a scale of one to ten. Ten means you were totally focused throughout the swing. Then rate how well you sent your energy toward the target. That's all you consider. Don't worry at all about what went wrong. After an undesirable outcome, take a review practice swing to remind yourself of the right swing, and go on to the next shot. Don't get mechanical when in Target Golf mode. That's the death of a golfer.

Commitment

To "just do it," you need to have your mind clear of all but the target to give your brain a chance to focus on the task at hand. The task at hand is to get the ball to the target, not to make a good swing. It is too late for mechanics at this time. Focusing on mechanics will only distract you from your target. Commit to the target by focusing on it while you swing, and more of your shots will fly there.

Your commitment to golf in general includes regular and intelligent practice in both Golf Swing mode and Target Golf mode. As you improve, you should spend less time on your swing and more time on the target. Also, you should spend two-thirds of your practice time on your short game. Golf is all about self discipline. The word discipline originally meant "to lead." Lead yourself in the direction you want to go. If you want to get good, the information is right here for you. You just have to do it. It's that simple.

Confidence

You must have no doubts in your mind about whether you have the right club, or whether you can get over that water hazard or whatever. Your pre-shot routine will help your confidence because you won't swing until you have locked the target and are ready to go, but there is another important matter.

Don't try a shot you don't own. Practice shots on the range before you try them on the course. If you have a 230 yard shot over water to get to the green and you can only hit it 200 yards, don't hit the shot. Lay up to a position you can play from. Make every situation as familiar as possible by changing your target to one you know you can hit, and you will have reason to feel confident. It is true that you will, at some point, have to try a shot you are unsure of, and that's not a bad thing, but you want to keep those times to a minimum. When you try such a shot, you may have doubts in your mind while you swing. The key is to stick to your routine and trust yourself. When you hit a shot you know you can hit, you'll be more confident, and you'll put a better swing on the ball, so stick with your strengths.

About Hazards

Hazards are a golf course architect's tools which he uses to outline the best places to hit your ball. Hazards can cause you to lose confidence, but you can overcome them if you realize that they are only there to help define the target. When you see a hazard, you simply have to notice that it is telling you to pick another place to hit the ball. The more appropriate target may be short of the hazard, over the hazard, or to one side or the other. You must let the hazards define your target for you and then focus on the target. One major difference between good players and not so good players is that not so good players focus on hazards, while good players focus on targets.

Composure

You will not hit all of your shots perfectly, even if you go through the best routine in the world and have the best swing. You are only human, and as such you will make a bad swing from time to time. The idea is to *put your brain in gear to hit the ball well, and then accept the result and go on to the next shot.* As soon as you allow yourself to dwell on past shots, you will ruin your chances of playing good golf. This paragraph is way too short for the importance of the information it contains. You might want to read it a few more times. Thinking properly sounds so easy, but golf has a way of frustrating people, making them do, think, and say strange things that have little to do with playing good golf.

It helps to realize that one round of golf is not the only measure of your improvement. Even the best players in the world have bad rounds, and they are playing for a living and practicing all day, every day.

Let me get one thing straight: I am not saying you absolutely can't get angry, although it has been found that anger significantly changes your body chemistry for the worse. Composure can be summed up in this statement: Never hit a ball while angry or, in any other way, distracted from focusing on the target. If you hit a ball while thinking, "If I make par here, I'll shoot my best round ever" that's just as bad a mental error as hitting a ball while angry about the previous shot. In both cases, you are not concentrating on the shot at hand, which is the only thing that matters.

I remember playing a round of golf at a really good, challenging golf course in South Carolina. I had been hitting the ball out to the right all day, but had managed enough good shots and holed enough putts to be two under par going into the par five, eighteenth hole.

The ocean lines the right side of the hole and there are several high mounds with bunkers in between the mounds that divide the fairway in two. You can play left or right of the mounds, but you really don't want to be in them. The safe play is left of the mounds, and that's where I had intended to hit my drive, only the ball went right (again) and into the mounds. When I found the ball, it lay in one of the bunkers so that I could not see the golf course at all. I walked up to the top of the mountain of moguls to see where I should hit the ball, walked back to my ball in the bunker, and hit the shot perfectly to the one hundred yard marker.

Now, a one-hundred yard shot is just about my all time favorite. I believe that I can make the shot from there, although I rarely do. But this shot made me wonder a little. The hole was cut in the very front of the green, and the drop-off into the ocean was only about fifteen feet to the right of the hole. I went through my pre-shot routine, settled over the ball and then, just as I was about to hit the ball, "don't hit this to the right" flashed in my mind. Luckily, I had the presence of mind to back away from the ball and take the opportunity to chastise myself for my poor thinking. I reminded myself that I *owned* this shot. I focused on the target, trying to hole the shot, and hit the ball six inches from the cup. I had kept my composure and focused on the shot at hand. And it *worked*. That shot, although it didn't come in a tournament, stands out so clearly in my memory because it perfectly illustrated the importance of focusing my mind on the shot at hand.

Composure is simply having the presence of mind to control your thoughts so that you send your brain in the direction you want it to go. Golf seems to lend itself so well to negative thinking because you so seldom hit perfect shots. The playing of golf includes something I call "The Negativity Battle." You have to fight those negative thoughts and stay positive for the next shot. Keep your mind on the shot you are about to hit, not on the one you just hit or what you will do in the near future.

Let's look at few ways I know of to maintain your composure.

> Target Lock every shot. Don't swing until your brain tells you you're ready. If you find yourself thinking bad thoughts over the ball, back away and go through your routine again. Wait out bad thoughts until you can replace them with good ones.

> If you are overly pumped up, either positively or negatively, tighten up every muscle in your body as much as possible, and then just let go. While you let go, let the last shot go and move on to the next shot.

> Breath deeply in through the nose and out through the mouth.

> Squeeze the ball tightly and then let go. When you let the ball go, let the last shot go, too.

> Tie your shoes.

> Smile. Think of something that makes you smile. Try to laugh off bad shots. Your friends will think you're crazy, but they will probably be giving you their money at the end of the round.

Be careful of getting angry. I, personally, find that it seems to escalate if I allow too many negative reactions to results I don't like. You know yourself. If you can blow off a little steam without bothering anyone else and still be fully prepared for the next shot, you're in good shape.

There are days when nothing goes right. I firmly believe that there are days when your body just won't do what you want it to do. On these days, practice thinking the right things. You can always improve your mental game, even if your physical game is off. So take every opportunity to strengthen this most important part of your game.

Do your best by thinking correctly and practicing correctly. Sometimes your best for that particular day is ten strokes or more higher than what you usually shoot. That's OK, as long as you gave yourself the best chance to play your best. "Do your best" does not mean *play* your best. It means give your best effort. If you can leave the course or practice range and say you did your best, you can be happy. The best you can do is the best you can do, so don't get too excited. There are more rounds, and more tournaments still to come. Keep up your practice, both mental and physical, and keep plugging away. Don't ever give up.

A game of golf begins when you first take up the game, and ends when you stop playing for good. Take a long term view of your game. Unfortunately, you will only recognize improvement in retrospect. Let's put it this way. You are on the path to mastery of the game, and this path is never ending. You will never master the game, but that's not important. What you *will* do is improve for the rest of your golfing days. The *path* to mastery is where all fun is.

9
TROUBLESHOOTING

This chapter will help you find solutions to problems which may come up as you learn and play golf. Consult it whenever things start to fall apart. Usually, all you will have to do is go back to basics to reaffirm your fundamentals. Don't search for tips. Reread the appropriate section and make sure you are doing what you are supposed to do. Get yourself on video tape so that you know for sure what's going on. You may have to slow down and retrain. Keep in mind that, if you swing the club correctly, the ball has to go toward the target. You just have to make sure you do.

IF YOU FIND THAT YOU OFTEN MISS THE BALL COMPLETELY OR CONSISTENTLY TOP THE BALL:

1. Move closer to the ball and make sure your arms hang straight down from your shoulders. Check address position and balance.

2. Swing lower. Don't be afraid to hit the ground. Adjust. Get the feedback your brain requires by swinging too high sometimes and too low others. Don't allow yourself to make the same mistake twice in a row. If you top the ball on one shot, purposely hit the ground with the next swing. Adjusting equals learning.

3. Swing at the grass, trying to brush it with your club.

4. Practice hitting a tee.

5. Make sure you are staying in your posture as you swing, and are not straightening up in your back swing. This is called **maintaining your spine angle**.

IF YOU FIND THAT YOU HIT THE BALL FAT CONSISTENTLY:

1. You may be too close to the ball. Check your address position.

2. Swing higher.

3. Check that your legs are not collapsing on your down swing.

4. Try to keep your spine in the same place while you turn back and through. Maintaining your spine angle is extremely important to your ball striking.

IF THE BALL STARTS LEFT AND SLICES:

This happens because your club path is outside-in, and your club face is slightly open at impact. As you know, the outside-in path is caused by a faulty forward swing.

1. Check your grip and alignment.

2. Pick a more appropriate target. Remember the Adjusted Target? You may have to pick a target to the right of the actual target to get yourself to swing in the right direction. Are you sending your energy to the target?

3. Check overall body tension. Monitor your tension always, it can destroy your swing.

4. Make sure you **definitely** start the forward swing by extending back and down. If you do not get the club head behind you half way into the forward swing, you cannot swing out toward the target.

CHAPTER 9   TROUBLESHOOOTING 175

IF THE BALL STARTS LEFT AND HOOKS:

This almost the same as above. The club path is outside-in, but now the club face is closed at impact, making the ball start left and then curve further left.

    1. Check grip and alignment.

    2. Are you keeping the target in mind throughout your swing? Are you sending your energy to the target? Adjust the target to help you swing in the right direction.

    3. Once you get your swing going in the right direction, then work on your how much you rotate the club face through impact. Educate those hands!

IF THE BALL STARTS RIGHT AND SLICES:

    1. Your path is probably good, but your club face is a little open at impact. Make sure you are not "death gripping" the club.

    2. Check your grip. The V's should point to your right shoulder. The heel pad of your left hand should be on top of the club.

    3. Rotate the club face a little sooner into impact. Basically, your left arm is responsible for rotating the club, so try to roll your left arm over a little earlier.

IF YOU SHANK THE BALL:

A **shank** is a shot hit off of the hosel of the club and goes almost straight off to the right. The **hosel** is the part of the club head where the shaft is attached. The only way you can shank a ball is to be too close to it. You may have simply stood too close at address, or somehow during your swing, you moved closer.

    1. Stand a little farther from the ball.

    2. Check you weight distribution at address. You may be out on the balls of your feet. Your weight should be 70% on your heels.

    3. Try to feel whether you are leaning toward the ball as you swing. The cure for leaning in is to stand tall as you swing. Don't let your head drop down or drift toward the ball.

    4. Try to hit the ball off of the toe of your club, then try to shank it. Train your hands to bring the center of the club face to the ball. My favorite word is "adjust." Adjusting equals learning.

IF YOU CONSISTENTLY LOSE YOUR BALANCE DURING YOUR SWING:

1. Check your weight distribution at address: 70% on your heels.

2. You may be swinging too hard.

3. Make sure that you load your weight onto your right leg on the backswing. You may be straightening your right knee, sending your weight to your left foot at the top of the backswing in what's called a "reverse pivot." Remember that if you turn well, and maintain the flex in your right knee as you go back, your weight will *automatically* shift to your right leg.

IF YOU HAVE TROUBLE MAKING SOLID CONTACT WITH CHIPS AND PITCHES:

1. Check your setup. Remember stance left, weight left, shaft left and ball position to the right.

2. Keep your weight on your left foot throughout the motion.

IF YOU HAVE TROUBLE MAKING SOLID, CENTERED CONTACT WITH YOUR FULL SWING:

1. Don't worry too much. Keep making your good swing, and allow your phenomenally intelligent subconscious mind to find the center of the club face for you. You'll hit the ball just fine as soon as you have put in enough practice time.

2. Check setup. Balance is key. Just a slight loss of balance can throw your swing completely off.

3. Check ball position. It should be within two inches of the inside of your left heel.

4. Cover the club face with duct tape to find out exactly where you're making contact.

CHAPTER 9   TROUBLESHOOOTING

GOLF YOUR BALL

Now you have the skills necessary to play golf and you know just about everything you need to know. How good you get depends upon how well and how often you practice, and how often you play.

One of my favorite sayings is "Go golf your ball." What I mean by that, is go out there and hit the ball, find it, and hit it again until you run out of holes to play. When people ask me how I am playing, I often answer, "I'm golfin' my ball," no matter how well I happen to be playing. Have as much fun as you can. Chances are that you need to.

Remember the Rules of Right Practice.

When you are working on your swing, work only on your swing and ignore ball flight completely. It is best to work on your swing in front of a mirror until you can make a good swing repeatedly, and then put a ball down and let it get in the way of your good swing. Do not let the ball distract you from making your good swing. Swing toward the target. Send your energy, via the club head, toward the target. Then educate your hands.

You've seen people make great practice swings, only to do something completely different when the ball is there. Don't do that. Just make that good swing. You should, if possible, video tape yourself while hitting balls in order to see what's *really* happening in your swing. Use the same viewpoints as with the mirrors (down the target line and face on). If you are going to take a lesson, insist on being video taped. You will learn *so* much faster if you can see what you are doing.

If you need to work on contact, simply adjust. If you are topping the ball, adjust. If you are hitting it fat, adjust. It's not rocket science! Contact will come easily. The hard part of golf is shooting low numbers. Making birdies and eagles takes some work, but playing golf respectably well is easy. Put your time in and practice well, and you will get better fast.

By practicing properly, you will learn a good golf swing in about three weeks to six weeks of daily practice. You need only about fifteen minutes a day in this time period to make your good swing a habit. After your good swing becomes a habit, put the ball in the way and swing the club to the target, letting the ball get in the way. Then go to work on controlling your ball flight, that is, educate your hands.

When you play golf, leave your swing thoughts behind, and trust what you have trained. Eventhough you may feel that your swing is a "work in progress," you must trust it, in whatever state it happens to be, if you want to play good golf. Don't work on your swing on the golf course if you have any intentions of shooting a good score.

Your short game is going to be most important in lowering your score, so spend at least half of your practice time working on putting, chipping, and pitching, with a little time on sand play as well.

I sincerely hope that this book has helped you learn golf, and that I might have been able to help you enjoy your game more than ever. Thank you very much!

Go Golf Your Ball!!!

COMING SOON FROM GOLF BETTER PRODUCTIONS

How to Teach Your Children Golf

- Get your children started correctly

- Build their self esteem

- Give them a game they can enjoy forever

Also by John Dunigan

(cut here and return this portion with your payment)

For additional copies of Essential Golf:

See your local bookstore, or send $20.00 to Golf Better Productions, PO Box 1557 Hockessin, DE. We'll pay the shipping. Please allow four weeks for delivery.

Please send me ____ copies of *Essential Golf* at $20.00 each.

Name _____

Address _____

_____

I would also like to be added to Golf Better Productions mailing list ____

Golf Better Productions
Hockessin, DE